Masterpieces
from the Gianni Mattioli
Collection

Masterpieces from the Gianni Mattioli Collection

with essays by
Laura Mattioli Rossi and Emily Braun

Peggy Guggenheim Collection, Venice
Solomon R. Guggenheim Foundation

Cover
Giorgio Morandi,
Bottles and Fruit-bowl, 1916
(cat. no. 17)

Picture Editor
Sandra Rossi

The biography of Modigliani is reprinted from:
Vivian Endicott Barnett, *Handbook, The Guggenheim Museum
Collection 1900–1980*, The Solomon R. Guggenheim Foundation,
New York 1984. © The Solomon R. Guggenheim Foundation,
New York, 1984

The biographies of Balla, Boccioni, and Severini
are reprinted from: *Masterpieces from the Peggy Guggenheim Collection*,
Guggenheim Museum Publications, New York 1996.
© The Solomon R. Guggenheim Foundation,
New York, 1983, 1986, 1993, 1996

Table of Contents

Preface

*The core holdings of the Guggenheim Museums consist of a number
of great individual collections that have come to the Foundation
in the course of its history: Solomon Guggenheim, Karl Nierendorf,
Peggy Guggenheim, Justin Thannhauser, and Giuseppe Panza di Biumo.
It is therefore a great pleasure to welcome to this illustrious roll of names
what is probably the greatest collection of early twentieth century Italian
art still in private hands, the Gianni Mattioli Collection, which has
been placed on long-term loan at the Foundation's Venice branch,
the Peggy Guggenheim Collection, through the generosity and public
spiritedness of Laura Mattioli Rossi.*

*There are intriguing parallels between Mattioli's career as a
collector and Peggy Guggenheim's. Each of them flourished in the milieu
of the intellectuals and artists of the avant-gardes they were to collect for
a long period of gestation before their rather sudden decision to begin
accumulating their collections. Both conceived of their collections not as
objects of private pleasure but explicitly as a way of supporting and of
spreading the knowledge of contemporary art. Consequently they were
both determined that their collections should be represented exclusively
by works of the highest quality and that they should be historically
impartial. The history Mattioli set out to represent was that of all the
important Italian artists and avant-gardes from 1910 onwards. Like
Peggy, Mattioli chose the avant-garde as his departure point—in Italy
this meant giving primacy to the Futurist movement, from the* Manifesto
of Futurist Painters *of 1910 onwards. Both collections were formed
rather swiftly—Peggy's by 1942 (at least for her pre-World War II
holdings) and Mattioli's by 1953 when it was presented in Florence.
Both collections, though private, have enjoyed increasing international
fame, have been presented in many cities worldwide, and have been
accessible to the public since the early 1950s.*

*In addition to the Solomon R. Guggenheim Museum
and to the Guggenheim Museum SoHo in New York, the Solomon
R. Guggenheim Foundation will soon be inaugurating the Guggenheim
Museum Bilbao and the Deutsche Guggenheim Berlin. In this way the
Guggenheim Foundation has positioned itself as the leading international
museum institution dedicated to contemporary visual art, with a unique
capacity to respond to the challenging environment of a world*

transformed by new means of communication. The long-term loan of works from the Gianni Mattioli Collection strengthens the position of the Peggy Guggenheim Collection as a major component of this international project.

It is a source of pride to the Solomon R. Guggenheim Foundation that we are able to make available to an ever-larger public, and on a permanent basis for the first time again after a thirty-year interval, this group of masterpieces that Gianni Mattioli selected to represent the quality and the fire of the Italian genius in the visual arts early this century.

Thomas Krens
Director, The Solomon R. Guggenheim Foundation
September 1997

LAURA MATTIOLI ROSSI

Gianni Mattioli

"Milanese by birth and family, I have just turned twenty years. My father who is a teacher in the Municipal schools made me study classics through my sophomore year in high school. For family reasons I then had to fend for myself, and at fifteen I left school and took a job in a cotton company where I still work today. My years spent in commerce, instead of diminishing, perhaps by force of contrast, increased my passion for everything artistic and literary. All my spare time has been given over to improving my education and, almost without realizing it, I have begun to feel in myself the growth of a consuming passion for journalism which I consider among the most admirable manifestations of human thought. I began working with a small youth magazine and from September last I have worked as theater critic of the *Ambrosiano*." This was Gianni Mattioli's description of himself in 1925, when applying to the editor of *Il Popolo d'Italia* for a job on the paper and obtaining, a month later, the position of theater correspondent in London.[1]

Born in Milan on 29 November 1903, Mattioli spent his childhood in Via Senato 8, a few meters from the house where Marinetti lived.[2] He showed a precocious interest in Japanese art (hence for a figurative style that was poetic and evocative rather than realistic and mimetic), as well as a genuine passion for reading, which enabled him to acquire as early as 1914–18 a sound knowledge of modern Italian and foreign literature and to develop a great admiration for Gabriele D'Annunzio.

In 1918, following the separation of his parents, he was obliged to interrupt his studies and to take a job as an errand boy in a company specializing in the importation of raw cotton. This first contact with the job market was decisive for him to the point that, after a brief interlude of journalism, from 1926 onwards he was always to work in the cotton business, first as a salesman for others, and then in his own company. In 1918, prompted by his literary interests, Mattioli chanced upon Boccioni's *Pittura scultura futuriste* (published in Milan in 1914) in the local library of which he was a habitué; with his youthful and rebellious character he was instantly attracted to Futurist ideas. In the same year his interest in anti-academic, anti-naturalistic and expressionist art became tangible

Gianni Mattioli, c. 1945

in a definitive passion for modern painting: he spotted the reproduction of a Blaue Reiter painting in the window of a shop in Via Brera and became so enthusiastic that he convinced the owner of the shop to make him a present of it.

In 1919 Mattioli left home and, despite his extreme youth, participated in Gabriele D'Annunzio's Fiume campaign, enrolling as a volunteer in the battalion of the *Arditi* (assault troops). He returned to Milan in January 1921, and spent several years living the *vie bohémienne*, which was to be decisive for his future collection. He was bound by fraternal friendship to the poet and critic Raffaele Carrieri, with whom he would meet after the day's work to discuss literature and art, and to share the company of the intellectuals and artists who frequented the Galleria Vittorio Emanuele II. Soon after, Carrieri, who had moved to Paris, would be his informant about cultural events in the French capital.

Gianni Mattioli, c. 1915

In February 1921 Mattioli met Fortunato Depero at the Galleria Centrale d'Arte Moretti on the occasion of Depero's solo exhibition, and he at once became an enthusiast of his work. Depero gave him a small *Selvaggetto* (Wild Man) in wood, and this episode marked the beginning of a friendship that was to last till Depero's death. It also initiated Mattioli's interest in the activities of the Futurists. Depero mediated between the first-wave Futurists and the younger second-wave intellectuals and artists who gathered round Marinetti after the First World War. Thus through Depero, Mattioli was linked to the group which was re-forming itself in those years in Milan: he came to know, among others, Giacomo Balla, Gino Severini, Luigi Russolo, and Luciano Baldessari, in addition to Marinetti himself. At the end of 1921, encouraged by Marinetti, he composed a few poems, "words-in-freedom" and a synthetic Futurist play. The following year Mattioli went with his friends to Turin for the "International Futurist Exhibition" in the Salon of the Winter Club (27 March–27 April 1922): a photograph shows him next to Depero and Marinetti (who sport waistcoats designed by Depero) and the playwright Francesco Cangiullo, with whom Mattioli shared his commitment to the theater.

In 1924, buoyed by his enthusiasm for the one-man show of Boccioni organized by Marinetti in the Bottega di Poesia in Via Montenapoleone, Milan (10–21 March), Mattioli attempted to convince a friend, a colleague from work, to lend him the money to buy some of the paintings on sale; but the friend, to whom Futurism was completely alien, was scandalized when he saw the exhibition and

refused to cooperate. Mattioli succeeded in obtaining only a few drawings, but his passion for Boccioni was to be decisive both for the acquisition of an important group of Boccioni's paintings by the City of Milan in the early thirties, and for his own future collection.

In those years between the wars Mattioli cultivated a variety of interests simultaneously: for Futurism, above all through Marinetti, who in 1924 invited him to participate in the Futurist Congress in Milan; for the theater, thanks to his friendships with not just Depero but Cangiullo, Russolo and Bragaglia; and for literature and journalism, through his collaboration with *L'Ambrosiano* and *Il Popolo d'Italia*. Remo Costa, from Rovereto and a friend of Depero's, recalled that Mattioli actively helped the Futurists in their relations with the press, by means of his friendships in journalistic circles.

In March 1925 he obtained the much-desired post of theater correspondent in London for *Il Popolo d'Italia*, but the trip proved fatal to his career as a journalist. When stopping over in Paris on his way to London, he ended up staying a month in the French capital, fascinated by the literary and artistic circles of the avant-garde to which he had been introduced by the Futurists. By the time he arrived in England he had been fired. He stayed through the summer working at the Italian Embassy, and returned to Milan in the fall, resuming both his work in the cotton business and his relations with the Futurists. Among the latter were Umberto Notari (owner of a bookshop in Via Montenapoleone 27, designed by the architect Luciano Baldessari), Fedele Azari (aviator, *aeropittore*, writer and Futurist publisher active in both the commercial and publicity fields),[3] both of whom he had met in 1924, and above all Fortunato Depero. The Depero-Mattioli correspondence,[4] which began in 1924, became more frequent in 1926 when Depero, in Paris for the world exhibition of decorative arts and for the "Salon de l'art d'aujourd-hui" mounted in December, wrote to Mattioli commissioning him to find him an apartment in the Lombard capital in readiness for his return to Italy.[5] Depero's desire to settle in Milan, expressed several times in the correspondence, was never to be fulfilled, but Mattioli became instead his chief point of reference in Lombardy. Further correspondence with both Depero and Azari was generated in 1926–27 by the preparation of the "libro imbullonato" *Depero futurista*, published by Dinamo Azari in 1927, and when Azari purchased an important group of works by Boccioni from the artist's sister.[6]

Mattioli continued to frequent Marinetti, Balla, Prampolini, Dottori, Fillia and the other Futurists who signed the manifesto of *aeropittura* in 1929, but he did not subscribe to the "Second Futurism" and he was never to collect their works, with the exception of Depero. After Azari's premature death on 25 January 1930, Mattioli wrote to Depero (who had recently returned from the United States) on 17 December of the same year, that he had in his house Depero's portrait of their mutual friend, a number of copies of the "libro imbullonato" and two large sculptures ("due grandi plastici") by Boccioni.[7] This is further evidence of Mattioli's special interest in the sculpture of Boccioni. From the 1931–32 correspondence with Azari's heirs it emerges that Mattioli had sent them in Pallanza a gesso sculpture painted red, which can most probably be identified with *Development of a Bottle in Space (by Means of Color)*, the title that was given a sculpture in Boccioni's exhibition at the Galleria Sprovieri, Rome, in December 1913. Regrettably the work reached its destination "with the cupola split and the base chipped," and today it is lost.[8]

From the papers preserved in his archive, it becomes clear that Mattioli followed closely the national celebrations for Umberto Boccioni organized by the City of Milan in June 1933. In the wake of the interest in Boccioni's work generated by an exhibition in the Sala del Consiglio Segreto of the Castello Sforzesco, Azari's father Quintino wrote to Mattioli on 10 April 1934 offering him fifteen Boccioni paintings that he was ready to sell following the breakdown after two years of negotiations with the City of Milan.[9] Quintino wrote again to Mattioli on 29 April 1934, offering him, in addition to the fifteen paintings, a further nineteen, as well as thirty-two drawings and a sculpture.[10] The documents reveal that the purchaser of the Azari collection was to be the accountant Ausonio Canavese of Turin, who was anxious to attain the title of *commendatore*. In the event he was obliged to settle for *cavaliere*, and in exchange he donated to the City of Milan an important collection of Futurist works, including the Boccionis, on 17 October 1934.[11] The incomplete archival documentation does not reveal exactly how many and which works by Boccioni Mattioli might have acquired during these negotiations, but it is likely that they included bronze casts of Boccioni's *Development of a Bottle in Space* and *Unique Forms of Continuity in Space*.

From 1932 to 1937 Mattioli had an affair with a woman who was separated from her husband and as a result, after years of living a nomadic life in rented rooms, he went to live with her in Via Stradivari 7 in Milan: photographs of this house show rationalist furniture decorated almost entirely by Depero, with tapestries, cushions, and a few paintings such as *City Mechanized by Shadows*.

In the 1930s Mattioli continued to pursue his interest in contemporary art through enlightened dealers such as Gussoni and Barbaroux, and above all through Gino Ghiringhelli. (He carefully kept in his archive invitations to exhibitions of de Chirico's paintings held in April 1931 at the Galleria Milano in Via Croce Rossa 6, and in May 1938 at the Galleria Il Milione in Via Brera 21.) His main interests were in literature and the theater. But this was a period of silence and of meditation for Mattioli. Keeping himself apart from public events and official culture, Mattioli threw himself into his work, and this would enable him later to view with detachment the progress of Italian art between the wars.

In 1937, during a trip to Egypt with an Italian commercial delegation to the wedding of King Farouk, he met Angela Maria Boneschi, daughter of a well-known Milanese businessman, and married her in October 1940. The wedding marked a turning point in his life, precipitating his definitive commitment to art. From 1941 his friendship with Gino Ghiringhelli deepened and he became an ever-more assiduous habitué of the Galleria Il Milione. In the same period he made contact with the collector and industrialist Carlo de Angeli Frua, who lent him paintings for his new house such as *Lunia Czechowska in Profile* by Modigliani (present whereabouts unknown) and *The Sacred Fish* by de Chirico (now Museum of Modern Art, New York), and from whom he was later to buy important works of *pittura metafisica*.

Gianni Mattioli in his house in Via Stradivari 7, Milan, in 1936

In 1943, obliged to move to Meina (Novara) by the bombing of Milan, he tried his own hand at sculpture, but above all, distressed by the massacres that the Germans were perpetrating on Lake Maggiore, he forged a close brother-sister friendship with Fernanda Wittgens, art historian, cousin and contemporary.[12] Together they worked to organize escape routes into Switzerland for persecuted Jews, including the critic and collector Lamberto

Vitali. Mattioli's relationship with Wittgens was nurtured by their shared humanitarian project, with all its dangers, as well as by a sincere passion for art. This was later to assume a philanthropic aura of social conscience in their determination to emancipate Italian art from its isolation in the Fascist period and to establish for it the international reputation it deserved.

Mattioli's alliance with Wittgens was to be fundamental to the birth of his collection. As early as 1943 there is clear evidence of his intention to create an important collection based not just on personal taste for domestic enjoyment, but on a project to survey and summarize the history of modern Italian art. In this way the ignorance and inertia of public institutions with respect to modern art would at least in part be countermanded.[13] But only with the end of World War II was it possible to realize his ambition.

Having returned to Milan in 1946 and to a new house in Via Gabba 9, Mattioli added to the early nucleus of works by the Futurists with paintings by Carrà, Campigli, Morandi, de Pisis, Funi, Sironi, Tosi and de Chirico, and with sculptures by Arturo Martini, Manzù and Marino Marini. Between 1947 and 1948 he rented a part of the studio of the painter Arturo Tosi, in Via Principe Amedeo 5, for storing the rapidly-growing numbers of paintings, drawings and sculptures for which there was no longer room in his home.

Those early years after World War II were highly productive for Mattioli. During the war he had succeeded in maintaining contact with foreign cotton manufacturers as well as with the few textile companies still active in Italy. In 1944 he founded a raw cotton import company of his own, which thanks to the rapid resurgence of the Italian economy in the immediate post-war years became the leader in its field. Professional success rewarded him with the means to form his collection and at the same time to travel frequently to the United States, where he was able to visit museums and become acquainted with important galleries of modern art.

Despite his intense commitment to his work, Mattioli's relations with Italian artists multiplied—with Campigli, Carrà, Manzù, Marini, Morandi and Sironi. His reputation as a collector spread. In 1946 he resumed his friendship with Depero, from whom he acquired practically his entire production before 1930, and through Depero he re-established contact with old friends such as Raffaelle Carrieri, Margherita Sarfatti, the Marinetti family, and the widow of Russolo. But in order to obtain the "historic" works which he believed were crucial to his *musée imaginaire* he turned to dealers: Barbaroux, Romeo Toninelli, Carlo Cardazzo, and Ghiringhelli.[14] He even founded a company with Ghiringhelli, the *G & G*, which between 1952 and 1954, through financial participation in the Galleria Il Milione, enabled him to acquire works such as *Dynamism of a Cyclist* by Boccioni, *Pursuit* by Carrà, and

The Solidity of Fog by Russolo (cat. nos. 5, 9, 21).

The most important addition to the collection came in May 1949, when Mattioli acquired *en bloc* the collection of the Brescian lawyer Pietro Feroldi through the mediation of Fernanda Wittgens and Gino Ghiringhelli. This was one of the most important collections then existing in Italy. It had been exhibited in 1933–34 at the Galleria Il Milione, Milan, and included first-rate works of Italian painting from the period 1910–30, as well as French drawings and paintings, mainly of the Post-Impressionists.[15] As Guido Piovene rightly pointed out in the preface to his monograph published by Edizioni del Milione in 1942, the Feroldi collection had been formed on the basis of historic criteria aimed at defining Italian art in its dialectic relations with French painting.[16] This approach interested Mattioli greatly, but in the light of his own experience he set out to give greater weight to the avant-gardes, and to Futurism in particular. The Feroldi collection included seventy-nine paintings and eight sculptures, but within two years (having rigorously selected only those works he wished to add to the nucleus of his own collection), only a few over thirty works remained, including *The Engineer's Mistress* by Carrà, *Landscape* (1914) and *Bottles and Fruit-bowl* (1916) both by Morandi, and *The White Horse* by Sironi (cat. nos. 10, 15, 17, 24).

Meanwhile the purchase of Futurist works proceeded apace: on 19 December 1949 Boccioni's *Materia* was acquired from Romeo Toninelli, after a protracted negotiation with the help of Depero going back to 1946 (cat. no. 4).[17] In 1950 Mattioli purchased Balla's *Paths of Movement + Dynamic Sequences* and *Mercury Passing Before the Sun* directly from the artist (cat. nos. 1, 2). He found Carrà's *Interventionist Demonstration* in the Galleria Bolzani in Milan (cat. no. 8). Severini's *Blue Dancer* came from Toninelli (cat. no. 22), and

Sironi's *Composition with Propeller* from Dr. Poli in Milan (cat. no. 23). Carrà's *The Galleria in Milan* entered the collection in 1951 from the Gualtieri di San Lazzaro family, Florence (cat. no. 7), while Rosai's *Dynamism Bar San Marco* was purchased from Carlo Cardazzo in Venice, 1951–52 (cat. no. 19).

With the acquisition of this group of masterpieces, Mattioli established Futurism, the movement which for him marked twentieth century Italian art's definitive break with the past, as the basis of his collection. 1909—the year of the Futurist Manifesto—was to be the

starting point. He purposely excluded Divisionism, which he considered excessively realistic and rhetorical, with its symbolist or social themes. Consequently he not only refrained from collecting the works of the Divisionists, but he even omitted Divisionist paintings by Balla and Boccioni. Emblematic of this is Boccioni's *La Signora Massimino* which belonged to Mattioli from 1952 to 1959 but which was never published nor listed in the collection.[18] The only exceptions to Mattioli's *terminus post quem* of 1909 were the sculptures of Medardo Rosso, in consideration of Boccioni's admiration for this artist.

The purchase of so many important Futurist works, that were available on the Italian art market in the same years that Mattioli obtained the Feroldi collection, qualifies the Mattioli collection as more than just the enlargement of the already renowned

Gianni Mattioli and Gino Ghiringhelli at the country house in Casorate Sempione, summer 1951

collection from Brescia. It was a systematic attempt to document modern Italian art with works of primary importance carefully selected for their capacity to define and represent a series of historical moments. In addition to the Futurist painters, Mattioli added, for example, Modigliani's *Portrait of the Painter Frank Haviland*, bought in 1949 from Italico Brass (cat. no. 12), Morandi's *Flowers* (1913) and *Still Life with Clock* (1915), both of which came from the artist *via* the Galleria Il Milione (cat. nos. 13, 16).

Begun in 1946–47, the Mattioli collection can be considered already fully formed both in its parameters and in its primary masterpieces by 1953, the year in which it was shown in Palazzo Strozzi, Florence—the same venue in which, in 1949, Peggy Guggenheim's collection had been presented. In his preface to the catalogue, Carlo Ludovico Ragghianti lamented the obstacle to public awareness of modern Italian art represented by the yawning gaps in public collections, and he described the Mattioli collection as having been "brought together with the intent and in the spirit of an historian," for the purpose of "revealing the signposts of a culture, the connections and the distinctions of an historical process which underlies aesthetic individualities."[19] This ambition was underpinned by a sense of social responsibility, since "the museums, the galleries, the art exhibitions are a factor without equal in human and humane education. The experience of art, thanks to its condition of freedom from any contingency ... is a fundamental part of man's experience... The coherent and rigorous documentation of contemporary art—one of the fundamental forms of spiritual expression—is the obligatory task of every generation."[20] If Futurism had placed Italian art in the avant-garde of the international panorama, the advent of Fascism had isolated it, enclosing it within "a moat of incomprehension." Thus, "we must give to scholars," continued Ragghianti, "to artists, to the public, and to foreigners the appropriate instruments for understanding the manifestations of our contemporary civilization and particularly that of art, which in the first half of this century has been exceptionally vital."[21]

Social responsibility, therefore, presided over both the historic criteria and the aesthetic principles that guided Mattioli's choices and furthermore influenced his management of the collection, whereby he set out to spread the knowledge of modern Italian art. Thus Mattioli from 1949 onwards forwarded a series of projects that went hand in hand, for twenty-five years, with his custody of the collection.

In the winter of 1949, he rented an apartment in Via Senato 36 where his collection was to be available to scholars by appointment as well as open to the public, each Sunday morning, from 1950 to 1967. Between 1949 and 1950, Mattioli promoted and advised on the organization of important exhibitions of modern Italian art abroad: "Twentieth Century Italian Art" at the Museum of Modern Art, New York (28 June–11 September 1949), the "Exposition d'art moderne italien" at the Musée national d'art moderne of Paris (13 May–11 June 1950), "Modern Italian Art" at the Tate Gallery, London (25 June–31 July 1950) and "Futurism and Metaphysical Painting" at the Kunsthaus Zurich (November–December 1950).

Fernanda Wittgens in her studio in the early 50s

Mattioli and Wittgens worked closely together to further the knowledge of Italian art. While struggling to rebuild Milan's museums and in particular to reopen the Pinacoteca di Brera, which finally happened on 9 June 1950, Wittgens also organized exhibitions of ancient art to generate international awareness of the urgent need for the restoration of the Italian artistic heritage. At the same time she curated exhibitions of modern art to reveal the vitality and importance of Italian art in this century. The Paris and London exhibitions mentioned above were organized by the "Friends of the Brera" and Mattioli actively participated

both as lender and as consultant. With Wittgens and the publisher Christian Zervos he worked on a 1950 issue of *Cahiers d'Art* entitled "Un demi-siècle d'art italien," which was published in Paris and dedicated entirely to Italian art.

Mattioli was also an influential consultant for the purchases of modern art that characterized the activities of the city museums of Milan in the post-war period (together with major projects such as the re-opening of the Galleria d'Arte Moderna in 1949, the construction of the new Padiglione d'Arte Contemporanea designed by Ignazio Gardella and completed in 1954, and the restoration of the museums of Castello Sforzesco, inaugurated in 1956). These included the donation of Russolo's *Self-Portrait* by the artist's widow, the purchase in 1952 of Sironi's *Futurist Head* (1913) and, a year later, a second Sironi, *Composition* (1952), from the Galleria del Naviglio, and the purchases in 1952 of Soffici's *Lines and Volumes of a Person* (1912–13) and in 1954 of the same artist's *Bottle and Glasses* (1915).[22] In 1951 Mattioli himself donated a large painting by Campigli, *The Staircase* of 1929, to the city collections, and in 1952 he recommended that the city buy Modigliani's *Portrait of Paul Guillaume* (1913) from the collection of Adriano Pallini, refraining from buying the painting for his own collection.

Following Fernanda Wittgens' death in 1957, Mattioli sustained his commitment to modern Italian art with continual loans of works from his collection world-wide and by collaborating with some important works of scholarship: the two-volume *Archivi del Futurismo* (edited by Maria Drudi Gambillo and Teresa Fiori, Rome 1958–62), "Avanguardia a Teatro 1915–1955 nell'opera di Baldessari-Depero-Prampolini," an exhibition curated by M. Monteverdi at the

Museo Teatrale alla Scala of Milan (29 November 1969–10 January 1970) and "Fortunato Depero 1892–1960," an exhibition curated by Bruno Passamani in Palazzo Sturm, Bassano (July-September 1970).

Following the Palazzo Strozzi exhibition in 1953, the Mattioli collection was exhibited in Turin in 1959, on the occasion of the opening of the Civica Galleria d'Arte Moderna.[23] Next, under the sponsorship of the International Exhibitions Foundation, the collection was presented in a series of museums in major American cities from 1967 to 1969,[24] then in Belgium,[25] Denmark,[26] Germany,[27] and Spain from 1969 to 1971,[28] and finally in Japan in 1972.[29]

Mattioli struggled with heart disease from 1962 onwards and died on 14 February 1977. Ten years before his death, reflecting on his experience as a collector, he wrote: "As a modest water-diviner, I have tried to locate and to signal the underground streams from which come the waters of the tumultuous river of the painting and sculpture which, in the years immediately before the Great War, have changed the face and the present-day concept of art: a river which has flowed parallel with a large part of my life or at any rate with one of its most interesting moments, because it coincided with that of my youth."[30]

[1] Mattioli Archive, Milan, letter from Gianni Mattioli, February 1925.

[2] This biography is written on the basis of stories my father used to tell and on documents preserved in his archive. I have published a short biography of my father with the title "C'era una volta," in L. Mattioli Rossi (ed.), *Boccioni 1912 Materia*, exhibition catalogue (Galleria dello Scudo, Verona, 8 December 1991–16 February 1992), Milan 1991.

[3] For Fedele Azari see L. Collarile, *Fedele Azari–Vita simultanea futurista*, Trento 1991.

[4] The Depero-Mattioli correspondence is owned by the Mattioli Archive, Milan, while the Mattioli-Depero correspondence is kept in the archives of the Museo d'Arte Moderna e Contemporanea of Trento and Rovereto, Fondo Fortunato Depero.

[5] Mattioli Archive, Milan, Depero-Mattioli Papers, letter dated 3 October 1925.

[6] For the history of the Azari collection see M. Garberi, *Da Modigliani a Fontana–Disegno italiano del XX secolo nelle Civiche Raccolte d'Arte di Milano*, exhibition catalogue, Padiglione d'Arte Contemporanea, Milan, 3 October–8 December 1991, pp. 6–7.

[7] Mattioli Archive, Milan.

[8] Mattioli Archive, Milan. Letter from Pompeo Azari to Mattioli, 19 February 1932.

[9] Mattioli Archive, Milan.

[10] Mattioli Archive, Milan.

[11] M. Garberi, *op. cit.*, 1991, pp. 6–7; L. Matino, "Storia di un museo futuro," in *Musei e Gallerie di Milano, Civico Museo d'Arte Contemporanea*, Milan 1994, p. 18; L. Mattioli Rossi, *op. cit.*, 1991, p. 20.

[12] In 1941, Wittgens was named Soprintendente per le Belle Arti of Lombardy and director of the Pinacoteca di Brera. See G. Ginex, "Fernanda Wittgens e la 'socialità dell'arte' 1903–1957," in *Il Risorgimento*, 2 (June 1989), Milan; G. Ginex,

"Fernanda Wittgens," in *Atti del Convegno Donna Lombardo*, edited by the Istituto Lombardo per la storia della Resistenza, Milan 1991.

[13] Mattioli Archive, Milan, Angela Maria Boneschi, holograph will of 17 July 1943.

[14] Some of the more significant letters between Mattioli and Ghiringhelli were published by the author in L. Mattioli Rossi (ed.), *Boccioni 1912 Materia*, exhibition catalogue (Fondazione Antonio Mazzotta, Milan), 2 April–28 May 1995, Milan 1995, "Appendix 1–Documents," pp. 232, 235–37.

[15] "Mostra Protesta del Collezionista," *Bollettino della Galleria del Milione*, 20 (23 December 1933–4 January 1934).

[16] G. Piovene, *La Raccolta Feroldi*, Milan 1942.

[17] The story of the purchase of *Materia* was published by this author in *op. cit.*, 1995, pp. 22–3, 231–37.

[18] Boccioni's *La Signora Massimino* was exhibited in Rome in 1953 in the same months in which the collection was being presented to the public in Palazzo Strozzi, Florence.

[19] C. Ludovico Ragghianti, *Arte Moderna in una Raccolta Italiana*, exhibition catalogue, Palazzo Strozzi, Florence, April–May 1953, p. 7.

[20] *Ibid.*, p. 31.

[21] *Ibidem.*

[22] L. Matino, *op. cit.*, p. 31.

[23] M. Valsecchi (ed.), *Capolavori di Arte Moderna nelle Raccolte Private. Mostra inaugurale della Civica Galleria d'Arte Moderna, Torino*, exhibition catalogue (Civica Galleria d'Arte Moderna, Turin, 31 October–8 December 1959), Milan 1959.

[24] F. Russoli (ed.), *Masters of Modern Italian Art from the Collection of Gianni Mattioli*, exhibition catalogue, The Phillips Collection, Washington, DC, 30 November 1967–14 January 1968. Subsequently: Dallas Museum of Fine Arts, Dallas, 1 February–3 March 1968; The San Francisco Museum of Fine Arts, San Francisco, 16 March–21 April 1968; The Detroit Institute of Arts, Detroit, 19 June–21 July 1968; The William Rockhill Nelson Gallery of Arts, Kansas City, 6 October–17 November 1968; The Museum of Fine Arts, Boston, 23 January–23 February 1969; Olivetti, New York, 5 March–5 April 1969.

[25] F. Russoli (ed.), *Maîtres de l'Art Moderne en Italie 1910–1935*, exhibition catalogue, Palais des Beaux-Arts, Brussels, 9 September 1967–12 October 1969.

[26] F. Russoli (ed.), *Italiensk Kunst–Gianni Mattioli Samling*, exhibition catalogue, Louisiana Museet, Copenhagen, 8 November–14 December 1969.

[27] F. Russoli (ed.), *Italienische Kunst–Sammlung Gianni Mattioli*, exhibition catalogue, Hamburger Kunsthalle, Hamburg, 19 February–30 March 1970.

[28] F. Russoli (ed.), *Maestros del arte moderno en Italia 1910–1935*, Museo Espanol de Arte Contemporaneo, Madrid, November–December 1970; Palacio de la Virreina, Barcelona, December 1970–January 1971; Museo de Arte Contemporaneo, Seville, January–February 1971.

[29] F. Russoli (ed.), *Masters of Modern Italian Art from the Collection of Gianni Mattioli*, exhibition catalogue, The National Museum of Modern Art, Kyoto, 15 April–21 May 1972; The National Museum of Modern Art, Tokyo, 31 May–9 July 1972.

[30] Mattioli Archive, Milan, typewritten notes by Gianni Mattioli, November 1967.

EMILY BRAUN

Renaissance and Renascences:
The Rebirth of Italy, 1911–1921

"To be great, Italy must be so in spirit, it must give life to a modern culture." Giuseppe Prezzolini, "The Re-Awakening of Italy," *La Voce*, 30 March 1911.

"To other countries, Italy is still a land of the dead, an immense Pompeii, white with sepulchres. But Italy is being reborn, and with its political resurgence will come a cultural resurgence. In the land inhabited by illiterates, schools will rise up; in the land of sweetly doing nothing, innumerable machines have already sounded their roar; in the land of traditional aesthetics, flights of inspiration are taking off, ablaze with the new." Umberto Boccioni, Carlo Carrà, Luigi Russolo, Giacomo Balla, Gino Severini, *Manifesto of the Futurist Painters*, 11 February 1910.

Although epic narratives are now out of fashion in the writing of history, the second decade of the twentieth century was arguably the most momentous for the development of modern Italy. Framed by the fiftieth anniversary of Italian unification at one end, and by the rise of Fascism at the other, the years 1911 to 1921 were inexorably shaped by events leading into and out of the Great War. The country was racked by one political crisis after another with a violence that signaled, in retrospect, the birth of a nation and, with it, modernist mass politics and a modernist avant-garde. "Something great is being born," wrote Giuseppe Prezzolini, the spokesman of his generation, "… but the intense labor is twisting the social body with spasms of pain."[1] The midwife in this long-awaited parturition was not the ruling class of moderate liberals, but a radicalized intelligentsia of writers, artists, philosophers and political theorists. And laying rival claim for the paternity of the new Italy was a triad of charismatic personalities: Gabriele D'Annunzio, Filippo Tommaso Marinetti, and Benito Mussolini.

Rebirth, regeneration, reawakening: the favored metaphors of the period may have been freely mixed, but they alluded to the same notion. Twice the progenitor of western culture, during the Roman Empire and again in the Renaissance, Italy had become impotent and obsolete compared to the rest of Europe. In the first decade of the century, Italy had enjoyed a belated economic and industrial boom, largely due to the dogged parliamentary politics of the Liberal Prime Minister, Giovanni Giolitti. Yet the visible advances in social modernization made the lack of a vibrant, contemporary culture all the more apparent. When the government passed a universal manhood suffrage bill in 1911, for example, roughly one-third of the electorate was illiterate, and there was little ideological coherence in a nation split between a wealthy industrial north and an impoverished south. The deep-seated inferiority complex and cultural despair shared by ambitious intellectuals born in the 1880s—the generation of 1914—insured the zeal, the religious fervor, with which they launched their campaign for national renewal.[2]

Rebirth, regeneration and reawakening are conventionally gendered as feminine terms, associated with procreation, organic growth and sexual coming of age. Yet the Italian avant-garde, like its European counterparts, was stereotypically masculine in its rhetoric, style and societal attitudes. Aggression, virility, steely resoluteness, the cult of war and violence, were necessarily opposed to the dissolute and sentimental, the passive and feminine culture of post-Risorgimento Italy. Although the women's movement and women writers made unprecedented advances during World War I, genius was unquestionably male, and even misogynist in the exertion of its creative will. As Marinetti put it, with a self-conscious gendering of prose: "Art has become action-art, that is, energy of will, aggression, possession, penetration, joy, brutal reality in art... geometric splendor of forces, forward projection."[3]

The debate over the modernization of Italy took place in the pages of the Florentine journal *La Voce* in the years 1908–11.[4] Led by the founding editor Giuseppe Prezzolini and by Giovanni Papini, the journal gave voice to intellectuals from all regions of Italy, united in their contempt for parliamentary democracy, bourgeois materialist values, and the compromises of reformist Socialism. Contributors included Benedetto Croce, the elder statesman of the anti-Positivist revolt, and Benito Mussolini, a young upstart in the internally-divided Socialist party. The painter and critic Ardengo Soffici brought readers up-to-date on Impressionism and, later, Cubism, and championed the work of a native son—Medardo Rosso—working in Paris. Texts on or by William James, Georges Sorel, Henri Bergson, Friedrich Nietszche, Sigmund Freud, and Otto Weininger accompanied editorials on sex education, women's issues, church, and school reform. Despite its scathing critique of the political establishment, *La Voce* did not align itself with any one oppositional party; in the words of Prezzolini, its agenda was "to bring culture into an ever more intimate contact with politics," to give it substance and practical application, and in doing so to reform the "national character."[5]

Above all, the intellectuals of *La Voce* recognized that only a new secular religion could unite a country fraught with regional and linguistic differences and with class strife. They were convinced of their élite role in the elaboration of this "modernist nationalism," of political rites and rituals that would bind the masses to the state.[6] Modernization had created material advantages but left a spiritual vacuum: a new sensibility had to be created that incited the emotions of the crowd. Faith in a strong, progressive Italy needed to be instilled through the creation of new myths and collective beliefs, through a

Marinetti in his house at Corso Venezia, Milan. Behind him is Russolo's *The Solidity of Fog*, 1912. Courtesy of Luce Marinetti

system of compelling images culled from historical tradition as well as modern technology. Indeed, much of the nationalist rhetoric claimed the preeminence of Italian genius in the future, based on the glorious creative achievements of the past.

The drive for renewal and elaboration of a mass culture were essentially modernist projects, but its forms of expression were not always avant-garde, if by avant-garde we mean a polemical break with the past, innovative formal language, and truck with a mass, consumer culture. At the beginning *La Voce* was dominated by a pragmatic style and by reasoned critiques, evident in its tolerance of divergent views. By 1911, however, an alternative modernism celebrating instinct and irrationalism was on the rise. The colonial conquest of Libya in 1911–12 and the ascendancy of the Milanese Futurist group signaled a shift towards a more radical agenda. In January 1913, Papini and Soffici split from *La Voce*, and founded their own journal *Lacerba* to accommodate their anarchic-individualist, transgressive posturing. Avant-garde aesthetics now joined hands with avant-garde politics. Reformist Socialism, once inspired by scientific Positivism, was now overwhelmed by the demand for violent revolution, led by a spiritual élite. In no other European country in the years before World War I was the avant-garde so committed to cultural militancy, to the use of art in the service of the state. As a result, the Italian pre-war avant-garde bequeathed aesthetic and symbolic forms, strategies of persuasion, and extremist rhetoric to post-war totalitarianism.

Against this background of strident nationalism and anti-Socialist, anti-democratic sentiments, 1911–21 was a decade of unprecedented cultural vitality, particularly in the visual arts. For the first time, Italy produced two movements of international clout, Futurism and *Valori Plastici*, which dominated the first and second half of the decade respectively. The activities of Futurism went far beyond the traditional fine arts and it was as much a literary movement as an artistic one. Nonetheless, aside from the individual figure of Marinetti, it was the Futurist painters—Giacomo Balla, Umberto Boccioni, Carlo Carrà, Gino Severini and Luigi Russolo—who achieved notoriety at home and abroad in the years around World War I. The activities of the journal *Valori Plastici* (1918–21) constituted a briefer episode, less broad in scope; it involved the Futurist turncoats Carrà and Soffici, the young Bolognese painter Giorgio Morandi, and the de Chirico brothers, Giorgio and Andrea (Alberto Savinio), who had made their reputations in Paris before the war. Their style of "plastic values" was no less influential on twentieth-century art, especially in generating a modern classicism that opposed itself to the Futurist *élan vital.*

Though differences between the two movements outnumber the similarities, one common denominator remained: the making of an art that was both modern and patriotic, true to the integrity of the individual genius, yet serviceable in the education of the masses. In Italy, to be avant-garde meant not only to avail oneself of modernist aesthetics, but to engage them in the popular culture of nationalism. The Futurist usurping of Cubist abstraction—the interpenetrating planes of objects and anti-illusionistic space—was no mere exploration of autonomous pictorial values. Whether in poetry or oil on canvas, fragmentation and rupture were used to impart the myth of radical renewal, of Italy's future ascendancy based on complete rejection of the past. Conversely, for *Valori Plastici,* the return to modeled, tactile forms asserted the primacy of an inherently Italian style; as with the culture of ancient Rome and the Renaissance, the Italian "constructive genius" would dominate once again, especially in a postwar Europe bereft of clarity and order.

In the realm of fine art and literature, the Italian avant-garde spurned *fin-de-siècle* aestheticism associated with the overwrought prose and decadent mythologies of Gabriele D'Annunzio. A figure of daunting literary achievement, D'Annunzio was an insatiable adventurer whose illicit conquests of women and the reading public both incensed and inspired the younger generation. One of the most influential promulgators of Nietszche and Wagner in Italy, D'Annunzio opposed the liberal parliamentary system and cultivated the political power of creative genius, the role of the poet-hero in inspiring national greatness. He impressed his personality onto the burgeoning industries of aviation and cinema, and rekindled the fires of Irredentism.[7] There was no denying D'Annunzio's contribution to the cult of a great Italy; yet the style of his art and life seemed hopelessly entwined in a *passéiste* sensibility, in aristocratic images of delicacy and refinement. D'Annunzio's writings found their visual expression in the languorous

Aristide Sartorio, *Ex Libris Gabrielis Nuncii Porphyrogeniti*, 1890. Sanguine etching. Fondazione "Il Vittoriale degli Italiani"

web of art nouveau line, the sheen surfaces of Salon painting, and in the supine, writhing bodies of his favorite painter, Giulio Aristide Sartorio. With their eyes typically closed or shielded from the light of day, Sartorio's figures submit to the enervating torpor of sensual pain and pleasure. In 1911 Sartorio had just completed his enormous mural commission for the Italian Parliament in Rome; to the younger generation, the empty magniloquence of his Michelangelo-inspired nudes, infused with Pre-Raphaelite effeminacy, symbolized all that was corrupt, not just with Italian art but with the collective image of the nation.

Poster for the "Esposizione internazionale," Rome, 1911. Museo Civico, Treviso, Salce Collection. Permanent loan, Italian State

The problem of the two Italys—of a cultural backwater in the process of accelerated modernization—came to the fore in 1911 with the "Esposizione internazionale" celebrating fifty years of unification. Conceived during Giolitti's tenure as Prime Minister, the Jubilee lauded the nation's economic progress and its acceptance into the modern European community. Nonetheless the self-congratulatory tone of the bourgeoisie irked many critics, who considered the government's achievements as insubstantial as the façades of the temporary pavilions. The myth of a unified Italy was undermined by the decision to separate the displays on industry and the arts, held in Turin and Rome, respectively. The fine arts section, in particular, drove home the retrograde quality of Italian culture, which had been held back by decades of regional polemics and by the lack of centralized and commercial infrastructures for the promotion of modern art. The organizing committee failed to bring about a retrospective of the previous half-century of Italian painting, which would have introduced the Tuscan *Macchiaioli*, the Milanese *Scapigliatura* and the northern Divisionists, to both a national and a European public. (These movements are still little known outside Italy today.) Furthermore, the display of contemporary Italian art, mounted in the new Galleria Nazionale d'Arte Moderna, promoted virtually all but minor artists from the older generation. (Paintings by Giacomo Balla and Felice Casorati were the exception.) As a result of the organizational gaffes even Sartorio refused to participate, and an exhibition of *Indipendenti* was organized in protest.[8]

The emphasis on certain international artists also demonstrated the time-lag involved in the reception of foreign trends. Italy was not without its informed critics, such as Soffici and Vittorio Pica, but the conservativism of both the Italian and foreign organizing committees understandably resulted in the dominance of Belle Epoque showmen like Ignacio Zuloaga and Anders Zorn.

Recent French painting was limited to a small selection of Monet, Renoir, Bonnard, Vuillard, and Signac, while Symbolism made its presence felt in the Belgian and Scandinavian contingents with the likes of James Ensor and Vilhelm Hammershøi. In 1911, as with the Venice Biennale the year before, Gustav Klimt and the Viennese Secession received the greatest acclaim. In sum, the younger generation of Italian artists were not yet looking to Expressionism, Fauvism or Cubism, but to overlapping currents of Neo-Impressionism, Symbolism and Art Nouveau, which were assimilated in varying degrees, region by region.

Alternative exhibitions, such as Ca' Pesaro, and the Roman Secession organized in reaction against official juried shows, represented a self-conscious effort to modernize Italian art; but here too, Fauvism did not make inroads until just before the war, and it was a tamed version at that.[9] In this context, Futurism appeared on the scene *sui generis*, revolutionizing cultural politics as much as artistic style.

Any incipient avant-gardism at the 1911 Jubilee was not to be found in the fine arts division, but rather in the exhibition of the *Agro Romano*, mounted off-site and in opposition to the official proceedings.[10] Organized by Socialist intellectuals devoted to the education of the peasantry, it documented life and work in the impoverished, malaria-stricken marshlands around Rome. The committee for the *Scuole per i contadini dell'Agro Romano* was actually the outgrowth of a feminist initiative begun in 1904, and included the novelist Sibilla Aleramo, the most famous figure of the women's movement, and her companion Giovanni Cena, a prominent editor and social reformer.[11] Along with Alessandro Marcucci, the director of the schools, the artists Duilio Cambellotti, Giacomo Balla, and others, Aleramo and Cena worked with government entities to improve livelihood and literacy, and to document the native populations and their artifacts. For the exhibition, Cambellotti designed a thatched hut, typical of the region, which contained an ethnographic display of tools and furniture. The interior was decorated with sculpture by Cambellotti and paintings by Balla, all inspired by the Roman landscape and peasantry, and rendered in Symbolist and Divisionist styles. While motivated by humanitarian concerns, these social activists looked to indigenous peasant culture as a source for their own creative renewal. The experiment with the *Agro Romano* on the part of intellectuals desirous of mediating between the state and the masses was one of the foremost examples of a socially conscious art, anti-bourgeois in sentiment and modernist in its appeal to a mythic primitivism.

Balla had signed the two manifestos of Futurist painting the year before, and was the only one of the five painters to participate in the "International Exhibition in Rome."[12] A decade older than the rest, he had already established a reputation as a painter of humanitarian–socialist themes. The absence of the Futurists was not surprising, given the heretical tone of their proclamations, and more importantly the fact that there was not yet a Futurist art to speak of. Balla, Boccioni, Carrà, Severini and Russolo still painted in a modified Divisionist style, using individuated brush strokes and color to "destroy the materiality of bodies." Their first collective exhibition, held in Milan in April 1911 (which included Boccioni's *The City Rises* [see cat. no. 3]) was met with derision by Ardengo Soffici, who exposed their ignorance of contemporary French Cubism. The Futurists retaliated with the first of many punitive expeditions, travelling to Florence to pummel Soffici in public at the famous café Giubbe Rosse; shortly thereafter, Soffici and Papini made peace with the Milanese, cultivating a shared style of provocation in the pages of the avant-garde journal, *Lacerba*.[13]

The first Futurist artwork, instead, was the original manifesto penned by Marinetti, that assaulted the readers of the French newspaper *Le Figaro* on 20 February 1909. That he made his statement in the cultural capital of Europe was indicative of Marinetti's cosmopolitan ambitions and his determination to counter perceptions of Italy as a slumbering nation. The "young and strong Futurists" aimed at nothing less than the overthrow of stodgy cultural institutions, the leveling of the old to make way for the new. More influential than the paean to modern technology was the activist rhetoric, the call to rejuvenate Italian culture with violent and incendiary means: "Take up your pickaxes, your axes and hammers and wreck, wreck the venerable cities, pitilessly." With a declamatory series of "for" and "against," Marinetti invented a new literary form, a collective statement of purpose that professed transgressive action over actual creation and traditional aesthetics.[14] "Except in struggle," he wrote, "there is no more beauty… Art, in fact, can be nothing but violence, cruelty and injustice."

Above and beyond its literary content, Marinetti's manifesto was a highly publicized event and a new form of hype. As Claudia Salaris has shown, Marinetti invented the avant-garde artist as entrepreneur, transforming the ivory-

The founders of *Lacerba* in 1914. Standing, from left, Palazzeschi, Papini and Marinetti; seated, Carrà and Boccioni. Archivio Giovanni Papini, Fondazione Primo Conti–Centro di documentazione e ricerche sulle Avanguardie storiche

tower intellectual into a shaper of public opinion.[15] Long before Warhol, Marinetti used his publishing house as a factory, working against the unique and the esoteric in favor of the multiple and easily available, while turning his publicly performed self into the ultimate cult object. Thanks to his financial independence, he was able to afford large print runs, and made a policy of giving away high numbers of complimentary copies, insuring an escalation of attention and demand. Creating works of art gave way to strategies of cultural production, as modernist practices of linguistic experimentation dovetailed with commercial advertising and mass distribution. Posters, leaflets, performances, and later the radio were strategically enlisted to choreograph the reception of Futurism amongst a diverse and international public. On the occasion of their first exhibition in Paris in 1912, for example, the Futurists' seemingly random antics and hostile denunciations of modern French painting were precisely calculated to provoke local artists and incite sensationalist coverage in the press.

The Futurists created the first interdisciplinary and global art movement, reaching beyond the traditional confines of painting and sculpture to embrace performance art, fashion, typography, film, even cooking.[16] Well before Dada manifestations, the Futurists invented the provocative happening, the incorporation of non-art materials, and the use of chance and improvisation as creative methods. They were the first to challenge the traditional values of uniqueness, originality and artistic labor. Having "destroyed the snobbish *passéism* of art-as-ideal, of art-as-sublime-holy-inaccessible," the Futurist artists

found their place "along with the butcher and the tire-manufacturer, the grave-digger and the speculator, the engineer and the farmer." They openly acknowledged the inevitable commodification of avant-garde production and rejected the false social consciousness of pretending otherwise: "The producer of artistic creativity must join the commercial organization which is the muscle of modern life. Money is one of the most formidable and brutally solid points of the reality in which we live ..."[17]

Taking their cue from Marinetti, the Futurist painters proclaimed a new subject matter of modern cities, machines, aviation, surging crowds, vulgar entertainment and mass communication. More to the point, modernity needed to be visualized through the "dynamic sensation" itself, through the multiplicity of physical, temporal and psychological states. To this end, they theorized an art that captured simultaneous experiences on canvas, a "style of motion" that merged instinct with mechanical rhythms and forms. By late 1911, Boccioni, Severini, and Carrà had adapted the faceted, interpenetrating planes of Cubism to depict the collision of objects and their environments, as well as the disintegrating forces of speed (cat. nos. 5, 7, 22). Balla and Russolo, instead, looked to the chrono-photography of Etienne-Jules Marey, which made visible in diagrammatic form the trajectory of movement over time and space (cat. nos. 1, 21). The profiles of moving objects were multiplied "like rapid vibrations" through a sequence of static points and blurred intervals running parallel to the picture plane. Futurist artists also used collage and mixed-media constructions to undermine the traditional unity and autonomy of the art object. The accelerated pace and fragmentary experience of modernity was reconstituted in the "dislocation and dismemberment of objects, the scattering and fusion of details, freed from accepted logic, and independent from one another."[18]

Marinetti, *Zang Tumb Tumb*, Milan, Edizioni Futuriste di "Poesia," Milan 1914. Book cover

As with the fine arts, the Futurist revolution in literature first appeared in theoretical form, orchestrating public reception with hype and anticipation. Marinetti's *Technical Manifesto of Futurist Literature* (May 1912) and *Destruction of Syntax–Imagination without Strings–Words-in-Freedom* (May 1913), attacked the conventions of grammar, narrative and the literary "I."[19] The printed word was to erupt with new "visual, auditory and olfactory sensations," through the play with onomatopoeia, emphatic typography and the imagistic arrangement of letters. Liberated from any connective logic, "words-in-freedom" would force the reader to make rapid-fire analogies between "distant, seemingly diverse, and hostile things." Marinetti compared the Futurist "imagination without strings" to the speed and economy of "wireless" telegraphic communication. It was in fact Marinetti's experience as a war correspondent that inspired his first published volume of words-in-freedom, *Zang Tumb Tumb*, in 1914. Based on the Bulgarian-Turkish conflict over Adrianopolis, two years earlier, it exploits word strings, various type-faces, and onomatopoeia to evoke the movement of trains and troops and the blasts of machine gun fire. Marinetti also performed *Zang Tumb Tumb* as a sound poem with variations in intonation, volume, facial mimicry and gestures. A *succés de scandale* all over Europe and Russia, Marinetti's performances served to propagate the Futurist cause, including the "communicative exuberance and epidermic geniality that is one of the characteristics of the southern races."[20]

The Futurist exaltation of motion, the mechanical, and simultaneity found its logical expression in cinema and filmic montage. Though in its infancy, Italian cinema was already, in the Futurists' opinion, "profoundly *passéist*," having lodged itself in the literary and dramatic conventions of the stage. The blockbuster of the period was *Cabiria* of 1914—a tale of sexual servitude against the backdrop of the Second Punic War—with captions by D'Annunzio, and featuring the strong-man Maciste, who went on to star in his own, immensely popular series of adventure films. Despite the ambitious statements of the 1916 manifesto, *The Futurist Cinema*, only a handful of Futurist films were actually produced, in part due to the exigencies of the war years, and lack of commercial viability.[21] The one extant film, *Thaïs*, by Anton Giulio Bragaglia with sets by Enrico Prampolini, begins as a conventional D'Annunzian melodrama of love and betrayal, focused on the eponymous *femme*

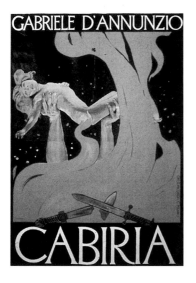

Leopold Metlicovitz, Poster for *Cabiria*, 1914. Museo Civico, Treviso, Salce Collection. Permanent loan, Italian State

fatale. But as Penny Marcus has shown, *Thaïs* is an allegory of the death of the diva genre and the birth of a Futurist cinema: the last few minutes of the film suddenly shift from a realistic setting to an abstract *scenoplastica*, that traps *Thaïs* within a spatial grid and stark geometric designs. The body of the diva is then immolated by the cuts of the camera and pierced by kinetic shapes in a kind of "abstractive surgery." Through montage techniques, *Thaïs* not only actualized the new filmic medium, but also "a double Futurist wish-fulfillment fantasy, bringing together the punishment of the transgressive woman with the exaltation of the all-powerful machine."[22]

The Futurist contempt for women must be understood as a direct attack upon the decadent stereotype of a seductive and sentimental femininity.[23] Informed by *fin-de-siècle* theories of biological essentialism, Marinetti perceived the predatory "nature" of women as a threat to male creativity, and to the virility of society. The denigration of the feminine as soft and passive was part of a larger ideological battle against bourgeois *mores*, but it also promoted a modernist aesthetic of streamlined, infinitely reproducible, non-organic forms. In a direct affront to church and state, Marinetti advocated casual and animalistic sexual encounters that would free both men and women from the burdens of marriage and family. At its most extreme, Futurist fiction unleashed the fantasy of a society completely free of the opposite sex, populated by self-procreating supermen, like Marinetti's own *Mafarka il futurista* (1910) who engenders a mechanical offspring. The dual burden of woman-love, decried Marinetti, "hinders the march of man, preventing him from transcending his own humanity, from redoubling himself, from going beyond himself and becoming what we call *the multiplied man.*"[24] Despite its apparent misogyny, the Futurist scorn for women had decidedly proto-feminist features.[25]

The editorial board of *L' Italia Futurista*, 1917. From left: Remo Chiti, Neri Nannetti, Bruno Corra, Emilio Settimelli, Arnaldo Ginna, Maria Ginanni, Trilluci, Marinetti. Courtesy of Luce Marinetti

In the pre-war years, Marinetti openly ridiculed the suffragette movement (which had made only limited advances in Italy through socialist and catholic women's organizations), but with the increased politicization of Futurism he cynically supported votes for women in the belief that this would accelerate the downfall of vilified bourgeois institutions and patriarchal structures: "Therefore I welcome with pleasure the aggressive entrance of women into the parliaments," cried Marinetti, "Where could we find a dynamite more impatient or more effective?"[26] By the time of the *Manifesto-Program of the Futurist Political Party* (1918) the movement promoted universal suffrage, a decisive anti-clericalism, quick divorce and the abolition of "marital authority"; in short, a genuine desire for the liberation of women and men from oppressive gender roles.[27] Marinetti's rhetorical posturing belied his actual record as a serious patron and publisher of women writers. During the war and immediately after, Futurism embraced women into its fold, especially as writers for the political mouthpiece of the movement, *L'Italia Futurista* (1916–18), which devoted numerous issues to feminist concerns.[28]

Marinetti's vituperative words had the merit of stimulating debate on women's rights, as well as spawning a literature both Futurist and female. Participants were drawn into a pre-constituted field of debate, either embracing sexual difference or proposing the virilization of the "weaker sex." In her *Manifesto of the Futurist Woman* (1912) Valentine St. Point refuted the binary opposition of the sexes, forwarding the precocious idea that masculinity and femininity were not biological traits but socially constructed ones.

By envisioning a new breed of warrior women, however, she also played into Marinetti's bellicose and phallocentric rhetoric. More original responses to societal roles and female subjectivity arose in the immediate post-war period, bolstered by the new-found freedoms and professional identities gained at the homefront. The author Futurluce observed that "rushing out of the house where the doll-women once reigned ... are the worker-women, the tram-conductor women, the carriage driver women, the cleaning women, the nurse women, the peasant women, the railroad-women and the clerk-women." [29] Mina Della Pergola and Maria Ginanni (who was also an editor of *L'Italia Futurista*, asserted their new independence with linguistic and thematic experiments that transgressed the social proprieties and patriarchal voice of conventional literature. Indeed, recent scholarship has argued that the Futurists Rosa Rosà and Enif Robert invented certain polemical strategies and a female "writing from the body" that anticipated the influential contemporary French feminists, Luce Irigaray and Hélène Cixous.[30] Yet it is also true that, once mixed with the strident nationalism of Futurism, the avant-garde discourse of female empowerment was readily absorbed into models of maternal fortitude and self-sacrifice later advantageous to the Fascist regime.

Although Belle Epoque images of graceful women with enveloping tresses linger in the Futurist Divisionist paintings (such as Russolo's *Perfume*, 1909–10, ex-Malbin Collection), it is curious to note the paucity of the female as subject after 1911. The exception is the Parisian-based Severini, whose series of cabaret dancers belong to a French avant-garde tradition (cat. no. 22). Futurist painting stands out from contemporary German examples, where the female body is brutally deformed in the name of gestural expression, or centered in a *lustmord* narrative of rape and murder. Even Cubist painting and collage created its bawdy jokes at the expense of a disassembled female anatomy. There is no visual equivalent to the anti-feminist, violent rhetoric of the Futurist literature, although the absence of women as subject could arguably be the result of intentional disregard. *The Technical Manifesto of Futurist Painting* rallied against the venerable tradition of the nude, because the subject had become as "tedious as adultery in literature." The authors' repugnance toward "unwholesome arrays of flesh" was less moral than sexist: the reproductive function of woman was, as Lucia Re writes, "the living reminder of man's biological destiny, and of his subjection not only to death and decay, but also to the evolutionary and genetic laws of an eminently conservative force: nature herself."[31]

In Futurist theory, the erotic charge of woman is replaced by that of the inhuman machine and the anonymous crowd, the dominating and the dominated. When the individual body does appear, it is resolutely masculine and in action: images of racing bicyclists and charging lancers, whose masses are refigured by velocity into mechanistic rhythms and sheath-like planes (cat. no. 4). Here the tactile volumes and interpenetrating facets of Cubism served the Futurists well, creating a visual dialogue between brute force and resistance, the disintegrating effects of speed and the inviolability of pure form. The breaking open of bodily contours refutes the limitations of the flesh, and visualizes a new unbounded self, celebrated by Marinetti in his manifesto on speed: *Velocity = scattering + condensation of the I.*[32] Oddly enough, the impervious figure of the mother frequently appears in the Futurist images of Boccioni (cat. no. 4). Either a sign of respect for matriarchal power, or a curious foil for the clashing of old and new, private and public, stasis and flux, her monumental presence unwittingly contradicts the Futurist claim for masculine power and self-sufficiency.[33]

Writing on the "Significance of Futurism" in *Lacerba* in 1913, Papini admonished against taking at face value what he termed the buffoonery and hyperbole of the movement.[34] Provocation was all a part of liberating intellectuals from the "superstitious" adoration of the past, and of extolling freedom in a country beaten down by slavish respect for the norm. Even the Futurists' exaggerated love of movement, continued Papini, could only be understood in the context of a country that perceived the world "as a train on a cluttered track, always running late." And despite the apparent influence of French forms, Futurism brought Italy up-to-date by creating an avant-garde movement competitive with the rest of Europe. Papini concluded that Futurism's weight was political: "… it has done more for nationalism than those who do nothing but pull out the Roman eagles and fall back on centuries of the Medici!" As Marinetti himself asserted, Futurism instituted a new form of patriotism, "a heroic idealization of the commercial, industrial and artistic solidarity of a people."[35]

In sum, Futurism can be credited with a variety of modernist and avant-garde practices, yet its significance on the whole has been marginalized in histories of twentieth century art.[36] The formalist approach favoring the development of abstraction and high culture, has ignored the Futurists' extra-pictorial interests, and categorized its fine arts production as a stylistic derivation of Cubism. While Cubism also embraced the lowbrow, with collage elements and musical hall referents, it did so as part of a modernist exploration of the linguistic and material properties of the medium that ultimately reinforced its hermeticism and cultural difference. Cubist investigations remained within the realm of private spaces and traditional institutions—those of the studio, private collector, the museum—whereas Futurism unleashed modernist practices into a variety of publics, media, and entertainment industries antithetical to the rare and precious. Cubism laid bare the mechanics of representation—how the conventional is made to look natural—which

Futurism then usurped as a sociopolitical tool of "perception management."[37]

Revisionist studies, in turn, while countering the formalist separation of style from historical context, have similarly side-lined Futurism, despite its paradigmatic agenda of cultural activism. For specific political reasons (its affiliation with Fascism), Futurism proves the embarrassing exception to the rule of a left-wing or liberal avant-garde.[38] In a now infamous essay, Walter Benjamin indicted Marinetti and Futurism for the introduction of aesthetics into politics,

for the nefarious use of mass psychology, violence, and spectacle in the formation of the totalitarian fabric.[39] Yet Futurism is the mother of modernist avant-garde movements precisely because it gave birth to the "art" of persuasion and the politics of mass culture. The Futurists transformed the subjective aesthetic experience from object to event, and, with it, transformed the status of the audience. Informed by the theories of Gustave Le Bon and Georges Sorel, they no longer perceived the "public" as a rational individual capable of active analysis, but as a passive spectator whose desires could be directed and controlled. The political value of the movement ultimately lay in its innovative and aggressive means of shaping public opinion, and not in its affinity with either left or right-wing ideologies. While accepting the demise of the traditional artist, the Futurists retained the privileged position of fashioning an image and, through it, reality. Above all, Futurism concerned itself with fashioning the image of a new Italy, a goal that sealed the movement's fate with Fascism.

The Futurist Lombard Volunteer Cyclists Battalion at the Alpine Front, 1915. From left: Marinetti, Sironi, Boccioni. The Beinecke Rare Book and Manuscript Library, Yale University, New Haven, Connecticut

Marinetti understood that capitalist laws of production and demand guaranteed the democratization of culture, as well as a new hierarchy of power. In his 1920 manifesto *Beyond Communism* he argued that mass culture would replace traditional religion as well as the new-fangled faith of Marxism. Once in power, the "vast intellectual proletariat" would organize free music, theater, cinema, books, and newspapers—entertainment and information in the streets, squares (and skies), at all hours of the day and night. The artistic patrimony would be toured, leased or sold abroad, as "dynamic transoceanic publicity" for the Italian genius. In tandem with developing technologies, intellectual and creative abilities would be multiplied and extendable to all. The fundamental purpose of art

(as with government) was to mask and relieve the mundanity, monotony, and harsh realities of material existence. In a statement that anticipates the means of modern advertising, Marinetti readily admitted that art was "...an alcohol. Not an alcohol that obliterates, but an alcohol of an elating optimism, that apotheosizes youth, multiplies maturity a hundred-fold and invigorates old-age."
He astutely observed that "the satisfaction of need brings pleasure," and where need cannot be fulfilled, "dream comes into play."
With the profusion of entertainment, diversion, and projected fantasy "life will become a work of art."[40]

The Futurists extended their ambition of merging art and life into direct political activism, beginning with their key role in the Interventionist movement. When war broke out in August 1914, the Italian government chose to maintain neutrality, a majority position supported by socialists and catholics. Yet the war was the moment of national aggrandizement, of a cleansing apocalypse that the radical left and right had been waiting for; it was, in Marinetti's words, the "necessary and bloody test of a people's force."[41] The campaign for intervention on the side of the Triple Entente (England, France, and Russia) became an internal conflict of youth against old age, the courageous against the cowardly, Latin genius against German pedantry. D'Annunzio galvanized the crowds with his compelling oratory, and the Futurists took to the streets with pamphleteering, performances, and the burning of Austrian flags.[42] In his "war paintings," Carrà deployed the disruptive syntax of collage and words-in-freedom to simulate the vocal and visual tumult of patriotic demonstrations (cat. no. 8), while Balla painted a series of abstractions based on unfurling flags and the psychological dynamism of the crowd.

L' Italia Futurista,
Florence, 25 August
1916. (With notice of
the death of Boccioni
and an image of
Balla's *Boccioni's Fist*)

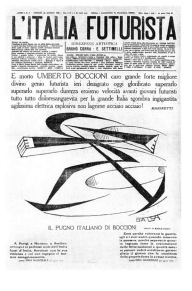

The Futurists allied themselves with a small but vocal minority of agitators: the Nationalists, revolutionary syndicalists, and renegade Socialists. Foremost among these last was Mussolini, who started his own interventionist newspaper, *Il Popolo d'Italia*, to propel the myth of national regeneration. Like D'Annunzio and Marinetti before him, Mussolini recognized the motivating force of rhetoric and representation, of packaging an idea with resonant symbolism and emotive charge. As a practicing journalist he was at the forefront in evolving strategies of press manipulation. "The young Mussolini," in the words of historian Robert Wohl, "possessed an extraordinary sense for the mood of the masses and the revolutionary possibilities of twentieth-century politics, based on his belief that reality was not a stable structure ... but a mobile, shifting, ever changing construction that could be dominated by the will of forceful men."[43]

When Italy finally declared war against Austria in May 1915, the Futurists enlisted as a group in the Lombard Volunteer Cyclist Battalion, where they saw action in the freezing trenches of the Alpine front. Russolo sustained serious injury, (as did Marinetti and Soffici), Boccioni died in a freak accident while exercising his horse at military camp and the visionary architect, Antonio Sant'Elia was killed in action. Italy lost 600,000 lives and endured the humiliating defeat at Caporetto, when enemy forces captured Italian territory in the Veneto. Meanwhile an even greater affront awaited those interventionists who had risked their lives for the love of nation: the peace conference dominated by Woodrow Wilson threatened Italy's long-held claim to Fiume and Dalmatia, and rebuked the country's ambition to international prestige once again.

War had changed everything but the promise of revolution, which it had incited even more. Balla's image of *Boccioni's Fist*—an ideogram of his late colleague hurling a punch—became an official logo for the movement, asserting that the artistic flank had lost none of its pugnacity. In September 1918, Marinetti announced the founding of the Futurist Political Party with the publication of a manifesto in the propaganda journal, *Roma Futurista*. He made a clear distinction between Futurism the art movement and Futurism the political party. While the former was dedicated to "the work of rejuvenating and reinforcing the Italian creative genius," he admitted that its avant-garde and polemical sensibility eluded if not offended the majority of the populace. In addition to a government based on labor unions, the Futurists proposed the "patriotic education of the proletariat" and the cultivation of "Italian pride."

According to historian Renzo De Felice, the co-mingling of nationalist, left-wing, and elitist agendas constituted the most significant expression of "that confused but sincere desire for radical political, social, and moral renewal" which gave birth to the Fascist movement.[44] The Futurist political cells soon joined forces with the unruly *arditi* or special assault troops, who were disbanded after the armistice. Together with Mussolini's revolutionary interventionists they formed the *fasci di combattimento*, on 23 March 1919, in the Piazza di San Sepolcro in Milan. Initially the *fasci* had no mass following, and were soundly defeated in the November 1919 general elections, even with Marinetti, Mussolini and Arturo Toscanini on the ballot.[45]

Gabriele D'Annunzio, instead, had garnered the political limelight in a decisive response to the "mutilated peace" of Versailles, which denied the Italian claims on the Adriatic: in September 1919, the poet hero occupied the disputed port of Fiume with a phalanx of some thousand black-shirted veterans, *arditi*, and Futurists, and with the tacit approval of the Italian military authorities who had previously administered the city. D'Annunzio declared Fiume a republic based on syndicalist corporations (including one for inspirational genius) and remained in place until forcibly removed by the Italian militia fifteen months later. The episode furnished a vivid example of life imitating art: D'Annunzio had already laid the mythic foundations of Italy's claim to the Adriatic in his popular Irredentist epic *La Nave*. First performed in 1908, the historical drama was reissued in a new edition, in operatic form, and as a film directed by D'Annunzio's son Gabriellino, all in the timely years 1918–19.[46] The occupation of Fiume, in turn, proved a prelude to the Fascist aestheticization of politics: the military regalia and rites, the rhythmic movements and chants of the crowd, the liturgy of a mystic and populist nationalism, and the leader as cult figure. As Adrian Lyttelton observed, "Against the pseudo-religious rhetoric of 'communion' and 'sacrifice,' reason had no defense. The politics of poetry defeated the politics of prose, and not, unfortunately, for the last time."[47]

The occupation of Fiume was the culmination of the *guerra-festa*, or carnival atmosphere which the Futurists had done much to invent and promote. But Marinetti and the Futurists were bit players in D'Annunzio's spectacle, and their presence caused some competitive friction with the *Comandante*. The following year Marinetti broke with the *fasci* over Mussolini's conservative turn, further marginalizing the Futurist position. Though Marinetti would return to Fascism in 1924, it was as an artist operating in a politicized culture rather than as an avant-garde politician. Futurism contributed much to the Fascist style and ethos, but its anarchic, libertine current, and the left-wing specifics of its political program, proved incompatible with Mussolini's opportunistic need to build a broad base of power.[48]

In 1919, some fifty artists, writers, and activists participated in the "Grande Esposizione Nazionale Futurista" in Milan: Futurism had successfully become a national force, with artists from all regions. The movement also embraced a variety of styles, from the plastic dynamism of Ottone Rosai (cat. no. 19) to the bold, flat colors of Depero's "dynamic Futurist decorativism" (cat. no. 11).[49] Yet Marinetti's retrospective preface implicitly acknowledged that the cohesive heyday of the movement had ended with the war; more specifically, the conspicuous absence of Carrà, Severini, and Soffici, signaled a breach within the artistic flank. Futurism had initiated a cultural renaissance based on the paradoxical means of avant-garde nihilism: creation through destruction. "They have destroyed, destroyed, destroyed…" commended Antonio Gramsci, "without worrying if the new creations produced by their activity were on the whole superior to those destroyed."[50] But the war had prompted a re-examination of conscience on the part of many Futurists, and a new moral imperative to build anew. While they still hankered after a great Italy, they now differed as to the degree and kind of cultural intervention. Soffici for one, had returned from the front "another

Giorgio de Chirico, *Evangelical Still Life*, 1918, published in *Valori Plastici*, Rome, II, nos. VII–VIII, 1920

man," and in the following years he refuted his earlier cosmopolitan leanings in favor of an art bound to the customs and landscape of his native Tuscany.[51] His canvases of 1915, with their watermelon and Chianti bottles emerging with brutal simplicity from a Cubist backdrop, anticipate his post-war regionalism and populist themes (cat. nos. 25, 26).

The reaction against Futurism began as early as 1915–16 with a series of paintings and articles by Carlo Carrà, that hailed the "construction of pure values" and a new spiritual content.[52] Carrà's sudden shift to "antigraceful" everyday objects, wrested out of the Futurist flux (cat. no. 9), was indebted to any number of modernist primitives—Rousseau, Modigliani, or Kasimir Malevich. He himself acknowledged his debt to the Italian masters Giotto and Paolo Uccello, whose monumental forms in miniature and spellbound immobility exuded a "magic silence." He renounced abstract art and the undue emphasis on originality, but warned against the revival of historicist classicism or the slavish imitation of the past. The Trecento and Quattrocento primitives provided a model both indigenous and modern, based on a Cubistic armature of stark pictorial volumes and masses. Carrà's analysis was undoubtedly influenced by the aesthetics of pure visibility, and by Bernard Berenson, who similarly attributed an heightened aesthetic experience to the accentuated "tactile" forms of early Florentine painting. To be sure, Carrà credited Cubist decomposition with having determined, in dialectic fashion, the pure pictorial values of line and chiaroscural modeling. Similarly he lauded the Futurists for having brought Italian culture up-to-date. But the tenor of the times demanded certainties rather than subversion, a new "weighty cubicity" and equally sonorous content needed to replace the insubstantial planes and flippant experimentation of the pre-war years.

Carrà found an example of an art both innovative and traditional in the work of Giorgio de Chirico, whom he met in 1917 in Ferrara, where they were both sent during the war. Together with de Chirico's brother, Alberto Savinio, and the young artist Filippo de Pisis, they briefly formed the school of "Metaphysical Painting," inspired by de Chirico's ironic classicism. While remaining in the realm of the figurative, replete with ancient statuary and architecture, de Chirico's enigmatic images were a radical break with traditional representation. In works such as *Evangelical Still Life*, de Chirico combined unrelated objects in incongruous settings, bringing into question their function and significance. By inverting the age-old system of linear perspective, he undermined its symbolic expression of reason and measure in favor of a disorienting, immeasurable space. The schism between his illusionistic, highly tactile rendering of objects and surfaces and the lack of any narrative logic metaphorically alluded to the loss of classical unity, to the irrevocable break between the present and the past. Rooted in the negativist philosophy of Nietzsche, de Chirico's art negated absolute values, from God and the State, to the modernist myth of progress.[53]

The prescient Soffici penned an article on de Chirico's art in *Lacerba* in 1914, but otherwise his work was virtually unknown in Italy until 1918, and then primarily through reproductions and essays in *Valori Plastici*.[54] By the end of the war, his influence was manifest in the work of a number of former Futurists, including Mario Sironi, all of whom adopted de Chirico's starkly modeled forms and wooden mannequin figures (cat. no. 24). Carrà usurped de Chirico's bizarre iconography in a series of paintings from 1917–19, but his writings of the period reveal that he used the style of Metaphysical painting to different theoretical ends (cat. no. 10). In contrast to de Chirico's ironic mode, Carrà genuinely believed in the redemptive powers of art. Moreover he aligned the style of plastic values with a nationalist agenda congruent with the pre-war discourse of Italian cultural supremacy. The new Italian art needed to supercede the hitherto dominant French currents of modern art, which were based on a positivist naturalism, on a privileging of the eye over the intellect. Not surprisingly, the French mode of fleeting visual pleasure was associated with the bourgeoisie, whereas modern Italian art resorted to the "plebian virility" of implacable forms and compact surfaces. For Carrà, Italians were the "race of great constructors," and the "Italian principle" had been the point of reference for every radical renewal in the history of western art.[55] Ultimately Carrà's conservative appropriation of de Chirico's potent anti-naturalism was more influential in the immediate post-war period,

Carlo Carrà, *The Daughters of Lot*, 1919, published in *Valori Plastici*, Rome, II, nos. VII–VIII, 1920

VALORI PLASTICI
RASSEGNA D'ARTE

ROMA · ANNO II N. VII–VIII · PREZZO L. 4

a fact that infuriated de Chirico and eventually led to a split between the two artists.

In the meantime, de Chirico and Carrà, Savinio, Soffici and de Pisis joined forces with the Roman artists Roberto Melli and Mario Broglio to launch Metaphysical painting on a national level.[56] They solicited the participation of Morandi, who had independently arrived at the investigation of pure formal values with his deceptively simple, highly-deliberated compositions (cat. no. 17). *Valori Plastici* was dedicated to contemporary art based on the Italian tradition:

Ardengo Soffici, *Ines*, 1920, published in *Valori Plastici*, Rome, III, no. V, 1921

in theory, not a negation of the avant-garde project of cultural renewal, but in practice, a re-examination of artistic constants which the Futurists had spurned. Though often interpreted as the Italian vehicle of the larger European "return to order," the journal was, in fact, a mix of linguistic experimentation and retrograde naturalist revivals, of cultural chauvinism and cosmopolitanism. Special features on synthetic Cubism, L'Esprit Nouveau and De Stijl alternated with unnaturally still-lifes by Morandi and bizarre interiors by Carrà, the premise being that all were informed by primordial "plastic values." Less reconcilable were the apparent contradictions within individual artists' works: de Chirico's earlier enigmatic scenes appeared alongside current neo-Renaissance pastiches, while Carrà's incongruous juxtapositions gave way to a bucolic archaism. Of all the participants, only Soffici, with his images of bare-footed peasant women in the kitchen, had clearly embraced a reactionary style of realist-naturalism, ideologically embedded in the Italian soil.

Like other small literary journals of the immediate post-war period, such as *La Raccolta* and *La Ronda* (which shared many of the same contributors), *Valori Plastici* found solace in the autonomy of artistic practice and a "return to the craft," after the upheaval of the war. By contrast with Futurism, these artists turned their backs on the mass media, technology, and gender issues, if not on the popular culture of nationalism. As early as 1914, the vital source of modernity was, as Carrà put it, the "simple artistic expression of our people"; the way to go forward was to delve into the "pure and primordial" origins of form.[57] Though the return to past styles contradicted the teleological drive of the pre-war avant-garde, nationalist sentiment had always been deeply rooted in Futurist ideology. Above all, Marinetti glorified the inherent (and therefore traditional) "creative genius of the Italian people." The presence of the former Futurists, Carrà and Soffici, guaranteed the continuity of militant idealism, of a belief in the aesthetic foundations and political functions of myth. Futurism and

Valori Plastici alike promoted an agenda of cultural imperialism and racial supremacy, based not on militaristic power or biological purity, but on intellectual might.[58]

Anti-democratic, anti-positivist sentiments also permeated the prose of de Chirico, Savinio, and de Pisis, furthering the notion that reality was but the creation of a dominant will. Equating the practice of art with anti-socialism, Savinio proclaimed the role of intellectuals in shaping the "marvelous elasticity of public opinion. … Even more than political consensus, [art] must impose and regulate a true and actual dictatorship in life." [59] At the same post-war moment, Marinetti called for power in the hands of artists—"the intellectual proletariat"—who would "resolve the problem of well-being in the only way possible, that is, spiritually."[60] The sense of entitlement played right into the opportunistic hands of Mussolini, who, many times in the years 1918–19,

Mussolini at the time of the March on Rome, October 1922. Archivi Alinari-Istituto Luce

as Savinio recalled, "projected the future in our presence, delineating a program in which we would have participated in the cultural as well as political renewal of Italy."[61]

The heterogeneity of *Valori Plastici* led to a divergent legacy, both innovative and reactionary, at home and abroad. On the one hand, the reproductions of de Chirico's pre-war work directly inspired the revolutionary dream painting of the French Surrealists, while Carrà's domesticated version of Metaphysical painting also gave rise to the uncanny style of Magic Realism in Italy and *Neue Sachlichkeit* (New Objectivity) in Weimar Germany.[62] On the other, the alliance of autonomous pictorial values with *Italianità* furnished Italian Fascists of the early twenties with a figurative style that was arguably both traditional and modern. By 1922, Margherita Sarfatti, the leader of the *Novecento* group, to which many former Futurists adhered, claimed that the new order and clarity in art had presaged the restoration of authority and discipline in politics.[63] Only Soffici, however, defended a thoroughly parochial painting, which was to a certain degree anticipated by Morandi's humble landscapes and still-lifes (cat. nos. 15–18). With the *Strapaese*, a grass-roots movement of the Fascist period, to which Soffici, Carrà, Morandi and Ottone Rosai belonged, "plastic values" became synonymous with the solid and simple moral values of the "Italian race."[64]

The program of *Valori Plastici* was most indicative of that suspended moment between revolution and reaction that characterized Italian culture and politics from the end of the war through 1921. The Italian economy was in a shambles, with no jobs for the returning soldiers, let alone for thousands of industrial workers suddenly unemployed after the closing of the armament factories. Peasants who had fought in the war started to organize for land rights and began to seize farms by force. Strikes and incidents of violence escalated in a situation of unprecedented social unrest during the "Red Biennium," culminating in the occupation of the factories in northern Italy by the workers in the fall of 1920. Though Prime Minister Giolitti managed to diffuse the explosive situation, the threat of a Bolshevik insurrection led to reprisals against the left from the center and right. Amidst parliamentary crises and lack of confidence in civil authority, Mussolini seized the opportunity, mobilizing his black-shirts, occupying government buildings in the provinces, and marching on Rome in October 1922. At the end of the month he was appointed Prime Minister by King Victor Emmanuel III. Immediately thereafter, Marinetti, Carrà, Sironi, and other activists issued their public declaration of support for the new premier: "The assumption of government by the young Italian Benito Mussolini signals, at last, the end of the mediocre mentality that has held back, for so many years, the foremost quality of our race: the excellence of artistic spirit. Infused with idealistic values, Fascism is applauded by all those who can legitimately call themselves Italian poets, writers and artists. We are certain that Mussolini is the Man who will know how to justly esteem the force of our art, dominating the World."[65]

The myth of regeneration common to both Futurism and *Valori Plastici* makes plain the irreconcilable positions inherent in the Italian avant-garde from its inception. Desirous of shaping a new national identity, Italian intellectuals nonetheless held the masses in contempt and claimed special status as an elite "spiritual aristocracy." Both Futurism and *Valori Plastici* invented forms and theory useful to the elaboration of political propaganda, while simultaneously defending their creative autonomy. After Mussolini seized power in 1922, the ebullience of modernist practices and myths gave way to pragmatic dictates of normalization and consensus. "The potent rhetoric of cultural renewal," as Walter Adamson argues, "ultimately played into the hands of Fascism, which, in need of intellectual credibility, appropriated this rhetoric and adapted it to more politically explicit, but also more culturally impoverished ends."[66] The child of retardataire industrialization and artistic avant-gardism, modern Italy was now to endure a most wayward adolescence.

[1] G. Prezzolini, "Parole d'un uomo moderno: la religione," *La Voce*, 13 March 1913, pp. 1–2.

[2] See Robert Wohl's classic text on the epoch, *The Generation of 1914*, Cambridge, Mass. 1979, especially chapter 5 "Italy: Giovinezza! Giovinezza!," pp. 160–202.

[3] Giacomo Balla and Fortunato Depero quoting F.T. Marinetti in *Ricostruzione futurista dell'universo* (Futurist Reconstruction of the Universe) 1915, in U. Apollonio (ed.), *Futurist Manifestos*, trans. R. Brain, et al., New York 1973, p. 198 (hereafter abbreviated as *FM*).

[4] *La Voce* continued to publish until 1916, although under different editors; in 1914 it became, under Prezzolini's revived leadership, an interventionist journal. The history of *La Voce* and its relationship to Fascism is discussed by E. Gentile, *Mussolini e "La Voce,"* Florence 1976, and W.L. Adamson, *Avant-Garde Florence. From Modernism to Fascism*, Cambridge, Mass. and London 1993.

[5] Unsigned editorial (Giuseppe Prezzolini), "La Politica della Voce," *La Voce*, 30 November 1911, p. 697.

[6] The terms "modernist nationalism" and the "sacralization of politics" have been established by Emilio Gentile in his definitive studies "Fascism as Political Religion," *Journal of Contemporary History*, 25, 1990, pp. 229–51, and *Il culto del littorio. La sacralizzazione della politica nell'Italia fascista*, Rome and Bari 1993. Gentile's arguments for the link between the pre-war avant-garde and Fascism are synthesized in "The Conquest of Modernity: From Modernist Nationalism to Fascism," *Modernism/modernity*, 1 (September 1994), pp. 55–87.

[7] The Irredentists—from *Italia irredenta* (unredeemed Italy)—advocated the recovery to Italy of the Italian-speaking districts Trentino, Trieste, Fiume and Dalmatia.

[8] *Esposizione internazionale di Roma, catalogo della mostra di belle arti*, Bergamo 1911; *Esposizione Artistica Indipendenti Mostra di Belle Arti. Catalogo delle opere esposte*, Rome 1911. Medardo Rosso was represented in the official exhibition, but not by his most significant works. There were no paintings by Giovanni Segantini, the other artist of international reputation. On the politics of the exhibition see G. Piantoni (ed.), *Roma 1911*, Galleria Nazionale d'Arte Moderna, Rome 1980, especially her essay "Nell'ideale città dell'Arte …," pp. 71–96.

[9] R. Bossaglia, M. Quesada and P. Spadini (eds.), *Secessione romana 1913–1916, Esposizione XI Quadriennale d'Arte di Roma*, Rome 1987; *Venezia: gli anni di Ca' Pesaro 1908–1920*, Museo Correr, Ala Napoleonica, Venice 1987.

[10] N. Cardano, "La mostra dell'Agro Romano," in G. Piantoni (ed.), in *op. cit.*, pp. 179–88. The humanitarian socialist roots of the early Roman avant-garde are documented by A.M. Damigella, "Idealismo e socialismo nella cultura figurativa romana del primo '900: Duilio Cambellotti," in *Cronache di Archeologia e di Storia dell'Arte*, 8, 1969, pp. 119–73, and *La pittura simbolista in Italia 1885–1900*, Turin 1981.

[11] S. Aleramo, *A Woman*, trans. R. Delmar, intro. R. Drake, Berkeley and Los Angeles 1980. As described by Drake (p. v), Aleramo's book "sent shock waves through the European literary establishment," when first published in 1906, and was "hailed in its heyday as the Book of Genesis in the bible of feminism." Aleramo's subsequent career is the subject of an essay by F.A. Bassanese, "Sibilla Aleramo: Writing a Personal Myth," in R. Pickering-Iazzi (ed.),

Mothers of Invention. Women, Italian Fascism, and Culture, Minneapolis 1995, pp. 137–65.

[12] U. Boccioni, C. Carrà, L. Russolo, G. Balla and G. Severini, *Manifesto dei pittori futuristi* (Manifesto of the Futurist Painters), first published as a leaflet by *Poesia*, 11 February 1910, Milan (*FM*, pp. 24–7), and *La pittura futurista. Manifesto tecnico* (Futurist Painting: Technical Manifesto), first published as a leaflet by *Poesia*, 11 April 1910, Milan (*FM*, pp. 27–31).

[13] W.L. Adamson, *op. cit.*, pp. 148–49.

[14] F.T. Marinetti, *Fondazione e manifesto del Futurismo* (The Founding and Manifesto of Futurism) (*FM*, pp. 19–24). On the Futurist manifesto as an art form of "violence and precision," see M. Perloff, *The Futurist Moment*, Chicago and London 1986, pp. 81–115.

[15] C. Salaris, "Marketing Modernism: Marinetti as Publisher," in *Modernism/modernity*, 1 (September 1994), pp. 109–27.

[16] The variety of Futurist activities is surveyed by Enrico Crispolti in several publications: *Il mito della macchina e altri temi del Futurismo*, Trapani 1969; *Ricostruzione futurista dell'universo*, exhibition catalogue, Mole Antonelliana, Turin 1980; *Storia e critica del Futurismo*, Rome and Bari 1986. See also C. Salaris, *Storia del Futurismo*, Rome 1985, and *Bibliografia del Futurismo 1909–1944*, Rome 1988.

[17] The quotations are taken from B. Corradini and E. Settimelli, *Pesi, misure e prezzi del genio artistico* (Weights, Measures and Prices of Artistic Genius. Futurist Manifesto) 1914 (*FM*, pp. 135–50). In one of the most precocious examples of using chance to create new art and destroy values of originality and genius, they write: "And why shouldn't one, for example, not, for example, dedicate oneself to creating objects out of pieces of wood, canvas, paper, feathers and nails, which, dropped from a tower 37 meters 3 centimeters in height, would describe, falling to the ground, a line of more or less complexity, more or less difficult to obtain and more or less rare."

[18] U. Boccioni, C. Carrà, L. Russolo, G. Balla and G. Severini, *The Exhibitors to the Public*, exhibition catalogue, Galerie Bernheim-Jeune, Paris 1912. English version from the catalogue of the "Exhibition of Works by the Italian Futurist Painters," Sackville Gallery, London, March 1912 (*FM*, p.47). On Marey, photography and the Futurists see M. Braun, *Picturing Time. The Work of Etienne-Jules Marey (1830–1904)*, Chicago and London 1992, pp. 291–316.

[19] F.T. Marinetti, *Manifesto tecnico della letteratura futurista* (Technical Manifesto of Futurist Literature), 11 May 1912, and *Distruzione della sintassi. Immaginazione senza fili. Parole in libertà* (Destruction of Syntax–Imagination without Strings–Words-in-Freedom), published in *Lacerba*, 15 June 1913 (*FM*, pp. 95–106).

[20] F.T. Marinetti, *Lo splendore geometrico e meccanico e la sensibilità numerica* (Geometric and Mechanical Splendour and the Numerical Sensibility), 18 March 1914, (*FM*, p. 157).

[21] F.T. Marinetti, B. Corra, E. Settimelli, A. Ginna, G. Balla and R. Chiti, *La cinematografia futurista* (The Futurist Cinema), published in *L'Italia Futurista*, 15 November 1916 (*FM*, pp. 207–19).

[22] P. Marcus, "Anton Giulio Bragaglia's 'Thaïs,' or The Death of the 'Diva' + the Rise of 'Scenoplastica' = The Birth of Futurist Cinema," *South*

Central Review, 13 (Summer–Fall 1996), pp. 63–81.

23 See B. Dijkstra, *Idols of Perversity. Fantasies of Feminine Evil in Fin-de-siècle Culture*, New York and London 1986; E. Showalter, *Sexual Anarchy: Gender and Culture at the Fin-de-Siècle*, New York 1990.

24 F.T. Marinetti, *Contro l'amore e parlamentarismo* (Against *Amore* and Parliamentarism), from *Guerra, sola igiene del mondo* (War, the World's only Hygiene), 1911–15, reprinted in F.T. Marinetti, *Let's Murder the Moonshine: Selected Writings*, R.W. Flint (ed.), trans. R.W. Flint and A.A. Coppotelli, Los Angeles 1991, p. 80.

25 The contradictory position of Futurism—at once misogynist and proto-feminist—is discussed by L. Re, "Futurism and Feminism," *Annali d'Italianistica*, 7, 1989, pp. 253–59.

26 F.T. Marinetti, *Contro l'amore e parlamentarismo, cit.*, p. 81.

27 *Manifesto-programma del partito politico futurista* (Manifesto-Program of the Futurist Political Party), September 1918, reprinted in R. De Felice, *Mussolini il rivoluzionario 1883–1920*, Turin 1965, pp. 738–41. The evolution of Futurist political thought in the movement's manifestos is discussed by De Felice, pp. 474–82, and Crispolti, *Storia e critica del futurismo, cit.*, pp. 183–214.

28 W.L. Adamson, "Futurism, Mass Culture and Women: The Reshaping of the Artistic Vocation, 1909–1920," *Modernism/modernity*, 4 (January 1997), pp. 102–6; Adamson notes, pp. 102–3, that Marinetti had already included many women writers and poets in his symbolist publication *Poesia* (1905–9), "at a time when women were almost completely excluded both from mainstream journalism and avant-garde reviews."

29 *Futurluce* quoted in C. Salaris, *Le futuriste: donne e letteratura d'avanguardia in Italia (1909–1914)*, Milan 1982, p. 139.

30 L. Re, "Futurism and Feminism," pp. 259–71, and "Scrittura della metamorfosi e metamorfosi della scrittura: Rosa Rosà e il Futurismo," in *Chroniques italiennes,* 39–40, 1994, pp. 311–27; C. Orban, "Women, Futurism, and Fascism," in R. Pickering-Iazzi (ed.), *Mothers of Invention, cit.*, pp. 52–75.

31 L. Re, "Futurism and Feminism," *cit.*, pp. 254–55.

32 F.T. Marinetti, *La nuova religione–morale della velocità*, (The New Religion-Morality of Speed), 11 May 1916, reprinted in L. De Maria (ed.), *Teoria e invenzione futurista*, Milan 1983, pp. 136–37.

33 Of course, Boccioni's complex and emotionally wrought relationship with his mother goes beyond a mere reading of the painting in the context of Futurist rhetoric. For a fascinating psychoanalytic interpretation of Boccioni's preoccupation with his mother's image and the significance of *Materia*, see F. Petrella, "La 'materia' inquieta e le sue trasformazioni. Appunti per una ricerca," in L. Mattioli Rossi (ed.), *Boccioni 1912 Materia*, Milan 1991, pp. 83–114.

34 G. Papini, "Il significato del futurismo," *Lacerba*, 1 February 1913, pp. 23–5.

35 F.T. Marinetti, "Destruction of Syntax–Imagination without Strings–Words-in-Freedom" (*FM*, p. 97).

36 E. Milman, "Futurism as a Submerged Paradigm for Artistic Activism and Practical Anarchism," in *South Central Review*, 13 (Summer–Fall, 1996), pp. 157–79,

charts the neglect of Futurism in standard texts on twentieth-century art.

[37] The term "perception management" is taken from S. Ewen, *PR! A Social History of Spin*, New York 1996. Ewen documents the theoretical origins of controlling public opinion and the techniques of media manipulation shared by corporations and governments alike.

[38] The key text in the revisionary view of the historical avant-garde is P. Bürger, *Theory of the Avant-Garde*, trans. M. Shaw, Minneapolis 1984. Bürger effectively dismantled the dominant paradigm established by Clement Greenberg and Theodor Adorno, which had made modernism and avantguardism synonymous terms and antithetical to the interests of mass culture. Although Bürger argues that the avant-garde is so defined by virtue of its attack on the institutionalization and autonomy of art, and its political commitment, he avoids discussing the Italian Futurists. Bürger's thesis is the springboard for A. Huyssen, *After the Great Divide: Modernism, Mass Culture, Postmodernism*, Bloomington 1986. Most recently, C.S. Blum, "The Futurist Re-Fashioning of the Universe," *South Central Review*, 13 (Summer–Fall 1996), pp. 82–104, examines the rhetorical devices of Marinetti to expose the relationship between its artistic avantguardism and its sociopolitical chauvinism.

[39] W. Benjamin, "The Work of Art in the Age of Mechanical Reproduction," (1936) in H. Arendt (ed. and trans.), *Illuminations*, New York 1969, pp. 241–42.

[40] F.T. Marinetti, *Al di là del comunismo* (Beyond Communism), Milan 1920, reprinted in M.D. Gambillo and T. Fiori, *Archivi del futurismo*, vol. I, Rome 1958, pp. 38–40.

[41] F.T. Marinetti, "Destruction of Syntax–Imagination without Strings–Words-in-Freedom" (*FM*, p. 97).

[42] On 15 September 1914, Marinetti and Boccioni staged their first demonstration at the Teatro dal Verme in Milan; on the following day they caused a commotion at the Piazza del Duomo and the Galleria and were arrested after burning eleven Austrian flags. From prison they designed the flyer *Sintesi futurista della guerra* (Futurist Synthesis of War), signed by Marinetti, Boccioni, Carrà, Russolo and Piatti, which was then republished in the manifesto *Guerra sola igiene del mondo* (War: The Only Hygiene of the World) 1915. In December Marinetti, Balla, Depero and Cangiullo created havoc at a gathering at the University of Rome, and the following April the Futurists were arrested alongside Mussolini in front of the Camera dei Deputati, the Italian Parliament, in what would be the first of several political collaborations. A summary of Futurism and the interventionist movement is given by Crispolti in *Storia e critica del futurismo*, *cit.*, pp. 193–97.

[43] R. Wohl, *op. cit.*, p. 172.

[44] R. De Felice, *op. cit.*, p. 475.

[45] Arturo Toscanini soon became a powerful anti-Fascist and defied Mussolini on numerous occasions by refusing to play the requisite Fascist song "Giovinezza" before concerts; see P.V. Cannistraro (ed.), *Historical Dictionary of Fascist Italy*, Westport and London 1982, pp. 537–39.

[46] I owe my knowledge of the film *La Nave* (begun in 1919 and screened in 1921) to my colleague Millicent Marcus. Her unpublished manuscript on the political significance of the film forms part of an interdisciplinary project, *Italy 1919*, with Lucia Re, Robert Wohl, and Emily Braun. This collaborative research

has been funded by a Getty Senior Research Grant.

[47] A. Lyttelton, "Society and Culture in the Italy of Giolitti," in E. Braun (ed.), *Italian Art in the 20th Century*, London and Munich 1989, pp. 27–8, and *The Seizure of Power: Fascism in Italy, 1919–1929*, London 1973. See also M. Ledeen, *The First Duce*, Baltimore 1977. Fiume was declared a free city with the Treaty of Rapallo in November 1920. It was annexed to Italy under the Fascists in 1924, and made part of Yugoslavia after World War II.

[48] The course of Futurist politics and its relationship to both the Fiume adventure and early Fascism is documented by E. Gentile, "Il futurismo e la politica. Dal nazionalismo modernista al fascismo (1909-1920)," in R. De Felice (ed.), *Futurismo, cultura, e politica*, Turin 1988, pp. 105–59.

[49] *Grande esposizione nazionale futurista. Catalogo*, exhibition catalogue, Galleria Centrale d'Arte, Milan 1919, with a preface by F.T. Marinetti.

[50] A. Gramsci, "Marinetti the Revolutionary," originally published in *L'Ordine Nuovo*, 5 January 1921, reprinted in D. Forgacs and G. Nowell-Smith (eds.), *Antonio Gramsci. Selections from Cultural Writings*, Cambridge, Mass. 1985, p. 51.

[51] A. Soffici, "Dichiarazione preliminare," *Rete mediterranea*, March 1920.

[52] C. Carrà, "Parlata su Giotto," *La Voce*, 31 March 1916; "Le Parentesi dell'Io," in *La Voce*, 30 April 1916; P. Uccello Costruttore," *La Voce*, 30 September 1916. See M. Fagiolo dell'Arco, "Carlo Carrà 1915–1919: The Wonder of the Primeval," in *Carlo Carrà: The Primitive Period 1915–1919*, Milan 1987, pp. 9–34, which also includes an anthology of Carrà's writings from the period.

[53] P. Baldacci, "Giorgio de Chirico, l'estetica del classicismo e la tradizione antica," in M. Fagiolo dell'Arco and P. Baldacci, *Giorgio de Chirico: Parigi 1924–29, dalla nascita del Surrealismo al crollo di Wall Street*, Milan 1982, pp. 14–78; W. Rubin (ed.), *De Chirico*, Museum of Modern Art, New York 1982; R. Barilli, "De Chirico e il recupero del museo," in *Tra presenza e assenza: Due ipotesi per l'età postmoderna*, Milan 1974, pp. 268–303.

[54] A. Soffici, "De Chirico and Savinio," *Lacerba*, 1 July 1914. The seachange in Italian art and the delayed reception of de Chirico's work is discussed by J.M. Lukach, "De Chirico and Italian Art Theory 1915–1920," in W. Rubin (ed.), *op. cit.*, pp. 35–54.

[55] C. Carrà, "L'Italianismo artistico," *Valori Plastici*, 1 (April–May 1919), pp. 1–5, and his preface in *Mostra personale del pittore futurista Carlo Carrà*, Galleria Paolo Chini, Milan 1917, reprinted in M. Fagiolo dell'Arco, *op. cit.*, pp. 169–70.

[56] *Valori Plastici*, Rome 1918–21 (facsimile edition published by Mazzotta, Milan, and Archivi d'arte del XX secolo, Rome 1969). In addition to the journal, *Valori Plastici* published monographs on and by its contributors, and circulated a traveling show of its artists ("Das Junge Italien") in Germany in 1921. P. Fossati, *Valori Plastici 1918–1922*, Turin 1981, provides a complete history of the journal and its contributors.

[57] C. Carrà, "Vita moderna e arte popolare," *Lacerba*, 1 June 1914.

[58] F.T. Marinetti, "Democrazia futurista," *Roma Futurista*, 11 May 1919, reprinted in A. Schiavo (ed.), *Futurismo e fascismo*, Rome 1981, pp. 93–5.

[59] A. Savinio, "Arte=Idee Moderne," *Valori Plastici*, 1, 15 November 1918, pp. 3–8.

60 F.T. Marinetti, *Al di là del comunismo*, pp. 38–40.

61 Statement published in 1945, reprinted in P. Vivarelli, "Savinio e la teoria dell'arte negli articoli di 'Valori Plastici'," *Ricerche di Storia dell'Arte*, 5, 1977, pp. 117.

62 For a survey of the enormous influence of de Chirico and *Valori Plastici* abroad see W. Schmied, "De Chirico and the Realism of the Twenties," and L. Rosenstock, "De Chirico's Influence on the Surrealists," in W. Rubin (ed.), *op. cit.*, pp. 101–9 and pp. 111–29 respectively. The key influence of *Valori Plastici*, particularly Carrà, on contemporary German art was acknowledged at the time by F. Roh, *Nach-Expressionismus-Magischer Realismus. Probleme der neuesten europaischen Malerei*, Leipzig 1925, especially pp. 76–7.

63 M. Sarfatti, "La pittura italiana alla 13a Biennale Internazionale di Venezia inaugura oggi a Venezia," *Il Popolo d'Italia*, 4 May 1922, and "Nei dodici mesi dall'avvento: L'arte," *Il Popolo d'Italia*, 26 October 1923, and her preface to the *Catalogo della Prima mostra del Novecento italiano*, Milan 1926, p. 11.

64 Although Morandi's art has traditionally been viewed as void of political content, and his reputation escaped the taint of Fascism, he was closely affiliated with the *Strapaese* group from the mid-1920s to the mid-1930s. For the subtleties and ideological ramifications of this affiliation see E. Braun, "Speaking Volumes: Giorgio Morandi's Still Lifes and the Cultural Politics of *Strapaese*," *Modernism/modernity*, 2 (September 1995), pp. 89–116.

65 G. Brunati, M. Carli, C. Carrà, B. Corra, E. Daquanno, M. Dessy, A. Funi, A. Ginna, S. Gotta, F.T. Marinetti, A. Mazza, Settimelli, M. Sironi and M. Somenzi, "Un omaggio a Mussolini di poeti, romanzieri e pittori," *Il Principe*, 3 November 1922, reprinted in M. Sironi, *Scritti editi e inediti*, E. Camesasca (ed.), Milan 1980.

66 W.L. Adamson, *Avant-Garde Florence*, p. 262.

Catalogue

Philip Rylands

Giacomo Balla

1.
PATHS OF MOVEMENT +
DYNAMIC SEQUENCES,
1913
Tempera on canvas board,
19⅝ × 27¾ in. (49 × 68 cm.)

The paths of movement in the title probably refer to the flight paths of swifts that Balla watched from a window in his attic room in Rome. These are conveyed by the graceful arcs of the four white lines, while the beating of their wings, illustrated here in repeated images of the swifts themselves, are referred to as "dynamic sequences." The time of day, suggested by the gray light and brown colors, is evening. The window is present in the painting in the forms of vertical slats and of striated, persian blinds. The zig-zagging tubular shape of a drainpipe marches diagonally across the painting.

This study led to one of Balla's most magnificent paintings, *Swifts: Paths of Movement + Dynamic Sequences* (Museum of Modern Art, New York), which was completed by September 1913. Balla's study of the flight paths and movements of swifts was preceded by his *Girl Running on a Balcony* (Civica Galleria d'Arte Moderna, Milan) and was followed by his studies of rapidly passing automobiles. In all of these, he based his images on the repetition of movements in evolving sequences, and was influenced by the chrono-photography of Etienne-Jules Marey, who used white lines on the black costumes of his models as a way of rendering visible the rhythmical and, incidentally, abstract progression of the action.

Compared to *Girl Running on a Balcony*, *Paths of Movement + Dynamic Sequences* represents a breakthrough from a rather literal repetition of form, expressed in a choppy pointillist manner, to a language of lines, shading and transparent planes to convey the general sensation of movement. It is likely that Balla knew of similar experimental paintings, with comparably abstracting results, being carried out the previous year in Paris by Kupka and Duchamp. An intriguing element peculiar to Futurist concerns is the sense that the swifts are in the foreground; hence the spatial relationship between the artist indoors and the motif outdoors has been inverted, or at least confounded. This rejection of traditional pictorial perspective connects Balla specifically to his friend Boccioni and to Boccioni's assimilation of French Cubism (see cat. no. 4).

Giacomo Balla

2.
MERCURY PASSING BEFORE THE SUN,
1914
Tempera on canvas board,
49¼ × 40 in. (120 × 100 cm.)

This large painting represents the definitive outcome of several studies Balla made following his observation of a partial eclipse of the Sun caused by the planet Mercury, which occurred on 7 November 1914. Balla used a telescope appropriately fitted with smoked lenses, and these may explain the tawny sienna and tan colors.[1] However it has also been suggested that Balla was aided by photographs by the astronomer Janssen, known to him through Etienne-Jules Marey, of an eclipse of the Sun by Venus in 1874.[2]

The eclipse takes place in the upper center of the painting, with a small circle, Mercury, encroaching on a large circle, the Sun. The dazzle of white triangles nearby can be explained as the impact on the naked eye as Balla looked away from his lens. The green cone may also refer to a specific retinal color effect experienced by Balla as he peered down his telescope. For the rest Balla was continuing his experiments in conveying the sensations of movement through space with the use of transparent planes, rectilinear and curving forms in what Marianne Martin has described as "a glistening, smoldering display of cosmic pyrotechnics."[3] Martin considered Balla's intentions in symbolic terms at a time when World War I had already begun but Italy was still neutral: "Balla was asserting the inextinguishable strength and purity of the sun, unaffected by the antics of lesser cosmic bodies, and thus he created a totally unpretentious but profoundly Futurist act of faith."[4]

[1] The telescope itself is reproduced in V.D. Dorazio, *Balla*, Venice 1970, n.p., fig. 132.
[2] G. Lista, *Futurismo e Fotografia*, Milan 1979, p. 41.
[3] M. Martin, *Futurist Art and Theory 1909–1915*, Oxford 1968, p. 200.
[4] *Ibidem.*

Umberto Boccioni

3.
THE CITY RISES,
1910
Oil on cardboard,
13¼ × 18¾ in. (33 × 47 cm.)

This is the definitive preparatory study, and the only one executed with oils, for Boccioni's masterpiece of the same title which was completed early in 1911. All the main components of the finished work, over three meters wide and now in the Museum of Modern Art, New York, are included in this vibrant small work.

The scene is a building site, during the construction of water reservoirs for cooling the electricity generating plant in Piazza Trento, in the suburbs of Milan close to Boccioni's home in Via Adige 23.[1] The subject is *Lavoro* (Work), the title Boccioni gave the painting when it was first shown, in Milan in the spring of 1911, at the "Mostra d'Arte Libera." Workers pull their weight with cart-horses, with huge unicorn-like bridles, tethered by ropes that haul excavated earth. Boccioni, in a letter to Nino Barbantini, described the painting as "a great synthesis of labor, light, and movement."[2]

The City Rises is exemplary of the attempt by Futurist painters to give visible expression to their two manifestos, the *Manifesto of Futurist Painters,* and the *Technical Manifesto of Futurist Painting,* that they had signed earlier in the year.

Boccioni resorted to a Symbolist treatment of his subject—the idea of human and animal labor, expressed in sweeping forms reminiscent of those of one of their avowed pictorial heroes, Gaetano Previati, and using pure colors in short, directional lines common to the paintings of Divisionist artists such as Segantini, Pelizza da Volpedo, as well as Previati and Boccioni's teacher, Balla.

The Futurist component rested primarily in Boccioni's choice of subject matter, the burgeoning modern industrial city, with smokestacks and suburban popular housing blocks, but consisted also in the tendency of light to dissolve form, thus effecting a fusion of figures and setting that corresponded to Boccioni's early intuitions of the ideas of Henri Bergson and of the "unanimist" poets based in Paris.

The vitality of this oil sketch, with its stabbing and thickly impastoed brush marks, conveys Boccioni's exuberant enthusiasm while he worked on this project, and was surely his attempt to make his materials expressive of the excited movements and Herculean efforts illustrated by the theme.

[1] See L. Capano, A. Negri, "Ancora su Via Adige," in *Boccioni 1912 Materia,* exhibition catalogue (Fondazione Antonio Mazzotta, Milan), Milan 1995, pp. 258–59.
[2] Quoted in E. Coen, *Umberto Boccioni,* exhibition catalogue (Metropolitan Museum of Art, New York), New York 1988, p. 94.

Umberto Boccioni

4.
MATERIA,
1912
Oil on canvas,
90 × 60 in. (225 × 150 cm.)

This vast painting, executed in July and August of 1912, and exhibited for the first time in February 1913 at the Teatro Costanzi, Rome, is the most ambitious project Boccioni ever accomplished.[1] Like a watershed, it divides his early Futurist paintings from his later, fully developed Futurist work. From his writings we learn that he was particularly sensitive to the philosophy of the Frenchman Henri Bergson, and Boccioni's title recalls that of Bergson's fundamental 1896 text, *Matière et mémoire*. Bergson set out to define the nature of consciousness in the changed modern world—a consciousness in perpetual evolution and in a state of subjective flux owing to the influence of mood, memory, and free association on the ongoing information of the senses, in particular the eye. Boccioni sets out in *Materia* to create a pictorial equivalent for a new mode of seeing, in terms of perspective, the description of form, and the relations between figure and environment.

The subject is a full-length portrait of the artist's mother ("mater"). She is seated in a room at her home in Via Adige 23, Milan, with a window behind her overlooking the Piazza Trento below. The metal railing of the balcony is visible across the middle third of the painting. To the left and right below the woman's knees, cornices and balconies from houses nearby are visible in fragments. In addition a bay horse trots to the left and a man climbs a staircase to the right. At the woman's shoulders chimneys, buildings, a columned porch (corresponding to the entrance to the nearby Besozzi Marzoli Mill[2]) and rays of light, reflected from the windows, press in on and invade the woman's body. The scene is dominated by the penumbra of a semi-interior in an early evening light.

The artist has merged the frontal view of his mother with his own visual impressions of the outdoors reflected from the window panes, when he replaced her in the seat before him. His task was to weld the diversity of objects and incidents, interior and exterior, into a single magnificent visual whole, and thus give tangible expression to his promise in the catalogue of the Futurist exhibition at the Galerie Bernheim-Jeune, Paris, to "place the spectator in the center of the painting." In this way Boccioni convulsed the Renaissance tradition,

expounded for example by Leon Battista Alberti, in which the artist, by painting what is before him, from a single viewpoint external to the space depicted in his painting, obligates the spectator to adopt a similar viewpoint. Boccioni later wrote: "For us the picture is no longer an exterior scene, a stage for the depiction of a fact. A picture is not, for us, an irradiating architectural structure, in which the artist, *and not the object,* forms the central core.
It is an emotive architectural environment which creates sensation and involves the spectator. ...We therefore maintain, unlike Cézanne: *the boundaries of the object retreat towards a periphery (the environment) of which we are the center."*[3]

The woman's hands are at the physical center of the oblong canvas(es).[4] More than anything else, these hands and forearms, resting on the woman's lap, impress us with the power of the image and its title, as a symbol of universal maternity and creative power. This traditional reliance on symbolic meaning contrasts with other elements which look forward to imminent developments in Boccioni's work. The hands are the most sculptural forms in the painting, massive and solid, and they illustrate Boccioni's claim at this time that he was "obsessed with sculpture,"[5] an obsession that was to lead to the exhibition of thirteen sculptures by him in June 1913 at the Galerie La Boëtie, Paris. Several of these, especially *Head + House + Light* (destroyed), also depicted Boccioni's mother and were derived from *Materia,* as well as from Boccioni's related painting *Horizontal Construction* (1912, Munich, Bayerische Staatsgemäldesammlungen).

The images of the horse and

the man, representing incidents taking place in the *piazza* below the house, are different in their forms from the rest of the painting. The inspiration for the man was Marcel Duchamp's *Nude Descending a Staircase No. 2* which Boccioni had seen at the Salon des Indépendants, Paris, in March 1912. In place of the intersecting architectonic planes characteristic of Cubism, transparent planes with radiating and arcing lines imply movement. This looks forward to the language Boccioni was to use for his studies of rapid movement in the second half of 1913, such as *Dynamism of a Cyclist* (cat. no. 5), by which time symbolic subject matter and topographical detail of the kind we see in *Materia* had been replaced by forms that expressed "the dynamic sensation itself made eternal" (*Technical Manifesto of Futurist Painting*, 1910).

[1] The painting was reworked by Boccioni in the lower left portion, probably between March and April 1913 prior to its second exhibition, at the Rotterdamsche Kunstkring (13 May–15 June 1913). See M. Rosci, "La materia e lo stato d'animo plastico," in L. Mattioli Rossi (ed.), *Boccioni 1912 Materia*, exhibition catalogue (Fondazione Antonio Mazzotta, Milan), Milan 1995, p. 47.

[2] The Mill itself, as well as the balconies of Via Adige 23, are illustrated in: L. Capano, A. Negri, "Via Adige 23," in *Ibid.*, pp. 256–57.

[3] Quoted from chapter 15, "Noi porremo lo spettatore nel centro del quadro," of Boccioni's *Pittura scultura futuriste* (1914), reprinted in Z. Birolli (ed.), *Umberto Boccioni. Gli scritti editi e inediti*, Milan, 1971, pp. 173–74. This analysis of *Materia* is indebted to L. Mattioli Rossi (ed.), *op. cit., passim*, especially M. Dalai Emiliani, "Dalla trasparenza della mimesi all'opacità della poiesis," pp. 65–82.

[4] The canvas, originally almost square, was enlarged by additions to the top and bottom during the painting's execution. These are visible to the naked eye. See G. Rossi, "Osservazioni tecniche sull'esecuzione di *Materia*," in *Ibid.*, p. 222.

[5] Letter from Boccioni in Paris to Vico Baer, 15 March 1912.

Umberto Boccioni

5.
DYNAMISM OF A CYCLIST,
1913
Oil on canvas,
28 × 36 in. (70 × 95 cm.)

This beautiful painting, with its silvery lights and its vortex of cones and fin-like forms, is among Boccioni's most accomplished studies of dynamic movement. Although the bicycle was first invented in 1818, it was not until the 1890s that the modern bicycle, with its diamond-patterned frame, roller-chain drive and pneumatic tires, had become established. The racing cyclist can be taken as a characteristic Futurist symbol of dynamic modern life—man moving swiftly through time and space by the propulsion of his legs enhanced by modern technology. This is the subject of Boccioni's 1913 painting: the dynamic fusion of cycle, figure (bent double over his handlebars with his backside in the air) and space in a single plastic form.

Boccioni wrote: "…What we wish to give is the object seen in its *dynamic becoming*, that is, to give a synthesis of the transformations the object undergoes in its two motions, relative and absolute. …This suggests to us the lines of force that characterize the object's potentiality and lead us to a new unity which is the essential interpretation of the object, that is, the intuitive perception of life."[1]

"Absolute motion" for Boccioni was, in the words of Rosalind Krauss, "the structural and material essence of the object—what one might call its inherent characteristics"; "relative motion" was "the contingent existence of the object in real space, as a viewer changed positions relative to the object and saw new groupings form between it and neighboring objects … also … the distentions and changes in shape that would occur once a figure at rest was precipitated into movement."[2] Thus Boccioni's artistic purpose in *Dynamism of a Cyclist* was to create a unique "sign" that would synthesize these two states of being.

Boccioni made innumerable preparatory drawings for the *Dynamism of a Cyclist*, in which a network of arcs (*linee-forza*) dominate the diagrammatic construction of the unified form—lines which in the painting are for the most part resolved into curving planes animated by the choppy, still Divisionist brushwork with which Boccioni gave such surface vitality to all of his mature work.

The painting was first exhibited in Florence, at the Galleria Gonnelli, November 1913–January 1914.

[1] E. Coen, *Umberto Boccioni*, exhibition catalogue, (Metropolitan Museum of Art, New York), New York 1988, p. 248. Quoted from "What Divides Us from Cubism," from *Pittura scultura futuriste* (1914) which Boccioni was working on in the latter part of 1913 when he painted *Dynamism of a Cyclist*.
[2] R. Krauss, *Passages in Modern Sculpture*, Cambridge, Mass. and London 1977, pp. 41–2. Boccioni's "Moto assoluto e moto relativo" was published in *Pittura scultura futuriste* (1914) and in *Lacerba*, 15 March 1914.

61

Carlo Carrà

6.

THE GALLERIA IN MILAN,
1912
Pencil and charcoal on paper,
14¾ × 8⅜ in. (37 × 21 cm.)

Signed and dated 1912, this is one of two known drawings for the painting of the same subject also in the Mattioli collection (cat. no. 7). The second is a slightly larger, schematic line drawing in the collection of the artist's son, Massimo Carrà.[1] Here Carrà has softened the pencil and charcoal marks, possibly with his fingers, to produce the tonal effects he would shortly replicate with his brush. Both drawings confirm that Carrà's composition and many of the forms were already decided prior to beginning work on the canvas. A modified chiaroscuro and chromatic pattern and a greater complexity of form across the whole of the finished painting, were a natural consequence of working on more than double the scale when he took up his oil paints.

[1] This is published in M. Carrà, *L'opera completa di Carlo Carrà 1910–1930*, Milan 1970, p. 88, no. 33b. It measures 42 × 26.5 cm.

...

63

Carlo Carrà

7.
THE GALLERIA IN MILAN,
1912
Oil on canvas,
36⅜ × 20⅝ in. (91 × 51.5 cm.)

This has long been considered one of Carrà's most accomplished Futurist works produced under the influence of Cubism. Ardengo Soffici praised it as a "plastic symphony in browns, reds, deep blues and silvery whites" and ranked it among the greatest Futurist paintings, while Roberto Longhi described it as a "cavern of quivering stalagmites" and one of "the most beautiful examples of the movement."[1] Carrà himself considered it "a culminating point of my artistic activity in that period."[2]

The subject is the Galleria Vittorio Emanuele II, a Milanese landmark by the architect Giuseppe Mengoni. Begun in 1865, and largely complete by 1867, it linked the Piazza del Duomo and the Piazza della Scala with a vast cruciform arcade covering shops and cafés: it immediately became the bustling center of Milanese commercial and cultural life.

Carrà had recently returned from Paris where he had gone for the opening of the Futurist exhibition at the Galerie Bernheim-Jeune in February 1912. Thanks to Severini he had made the acquaintance of Picasso and Braque. *The Galleria in Milan* is a thorough appropriation of their style of the second half of 1909—with its choppy brushwork, its broken planes, and its silvery blue palette tending to monochrome. Nevertheless the modern-life subject—the noise, the hurly burly, and the soaring dimly lit architecture of the Galleria with Biffi's café in the foreground— was characteristically Futurist. Passages of lilac and yellow give the painting a luxurious sense of an expensive interior-exterior.

Carrà's attempt to distinguish his work from that of the Parisian Cubists functions almost as a description of this painting: "We Futurists instead were trying to immerse ourselves in the center of things, in such a way that our ego formed with their unity a single complex. Thus we gave to the plastic planes a spherical expansion in space, obtaining that sense of the *perpetually mobile* that is peculiar to all that is alive."[3]

[1] A. Soffici, *Carlo Carrà*, Milan 1928, p. 7; R. Longhi, *Carlo Carrà*, Milan 1937, p. 9.
[2] C. Carrà, *La mia vita*, Milan 1943, p.189.
[3] *Ibid.*, p. 137.

Carlo Carrà

8.
INTERVENTIONIST DEMONSTRATION,
1914
Tempera and collage on cardboard,
15⅜ × 12 in. (38.5 × 30 cm.)

Carrà described this *papier collé* in a letter to Gino Severini of 11 July 1914: "I abolished any representation of the human figure because I wanted to give the plastic abstraction of civic tumult."[1] Painted a few days after the assassination of Archduke Franz Ferdinand in Sarajevo (28 June) and published in the magazine *Lacerba* on the day that Germany declared war on Russia (1 August), it was conceived in exciting times. The image was inspired by the vortex-like spinning of leaflets dropped from an aeroplane over the Piazza del Duomo of Milan. Although given the title *Dipinto parolibero (Festa patriottica)* (Free Word Painting [Patriotic Celebration]) in *Lacerba*, it later acquired the title *Manifestazione Interventista* (Interventionist Demonstration) by which it is generally known today. This refers to Marinetti's and Carrà's active support of Italian intervention against Austria in the Great War. Interventionism was to become an issue for them only later in 1914, after the opening of the Great War itself in early August.[2] A generic patriotic and anti-Austrian fervor (referred to in the Italian flags and words such as TRIESTE ITALIANO) seems no less important than the evocation of a rowdy celebration.

Parole in libertà (Words-in-Freedom) were a literary form, liberated from the rules of punctuation and grammar, devised by Marinetti and used in such publications as *Zang Tumb Tumb* of 1914, in which words in different fonts and different sizes are "let loose" across the printed page. References to music, the use of words and the repetition of letters onomatopoeically (EEEVVVIVA for example) evoke Russolo's performances of *Spirals of Intonated Noises* in Milan in May 1914.

The distance between *Interventionist Demonstration* and his Cubist masterpiece *The Galleria in Milan* (cat. no. 7) is best explained in terms of Carrà's own manifesto written late the previous year, *The Painting of Sounds, Noises and Smells*. Carrà rejected "subdued colors ... greys, browns and all mud colors," and extolled reds, greens, and yellows, "oblique lines," "the sphere, elipses which spin, upside-down cones, spirals," "subjective interpenetration of hard and soft, sharp and dull forms" and much else aimed at defining a boisterous Futurist synaesthesia of sights, smells and sounds.

Marianne Martin has described this as both "the most Futurist of all Carrà's works" and "his swansong to the movement," since his interest was already turning to the well-springs of *pittura metafisica*: early Italian painting and the art of Giorgio de Chirico.[3]

[1] See M. Drudi Gambillo, T. Fiori, *Archivi del Futurismo*, vol. I, Rome 1958, p. 341.
[2] See C. Carrà, *La mia vita*, Milan 1943, pp. 214ff.
[3] M. Martin, *Futurist Art and Theory 1909–1915*, Oxford 1968, p. 194.

67

Carlo Carrà

9.
Pursuit,
1914
Tempera and collage on cardboard,
15⅝ × 27¼ in. (39 × 68 cm.)

With the opening of the Great War, several of the Futurists, spurred by Marinetti, turned their attention to war subjects, even before Italy entered on the side of the French and British (May 1915). This collage depicts a galloping cavalry officer, with knee-length boots, red trousers and a cylindrical helmet.

The use of more or less pertinent newspaper clippings, both French and Italian, and stenciled letters, testifies once more to Carrà's close ties to Parisian Cubism. The horse is preceded by the letters JOFFRE, the name of the French General who won the Battle of the Marne between 5–12 September 1914. Beside the soldier's boots, the word Balcan... refers to the upheavals on the other side of the Adriatic from Italy.

Other clippings however (Cinemas and MORITZ, for example) strike a discordant note of entertainment and sport, and Marianne Martin has pointed to an element of ambiguity and irony, even Dada *avant la lettre*: "The horse, though shown in an active position, seems essentially passive, or even static: it is like a wooden toy, floating in soft, airy surroundings. Its red-trousered rider looks more like a jockey than a warrior."[1] The horse does indeed seem less in pursuit of the enemy than wading through encumbering garbage. The explanation may rest with Carrà's awareness of the force of irony already pervading certain Parisian art circles, and with his growing distraction from Futurist concerns in favor of "plastic values" and spiritual content that was to lead to his abandonment of the movement in 1915. This may explain the complete lack of three-dimensional effects in this work, with the forms all pressed forward to the picture surface, as well as the detachment of the horse's relatively pure silhouette from its surroundings, whereas central Futurist dogma would have demanded that the horse be "opened up" to the forces that impinge on it. This collage was reproduced by Carrà in his book *Guerrapittura* (Warpainting) which was published the following year.

[1] M. Martin, *Futurist Art and Theory 1909-15*, Oxford 1968, pp. 199–200.

68

Carlo Carrà

10.
THE ENGINEER'S MISTRESS,
1921
Oil on canvas,
22 × 16 in. (55 × 40 cm.)

This powerful and strange small painting, which formed part of the great Feroldi collection purchased by Mattioli in 1949, closes the period of Carrà's *pittura metafisica*, of which, together with Giorgio de Chirico, he was one of the chief exponents. A series of preparatory drawings for *The Engineer's Mistress* (the earliest dated 1920, some squared for enlargement), reveal the care with which Carrà plotted the composition.[1] The spare assembly of objects draw on the standard repertoire of de Chirico's and Carrà's Metaphysical images.

Although evidently a mere sculpture, the upright female head is invested with an aura of semi-consciousness, as if hypnotized—the eyes closed but the mouth open in readiness to speak. The preternaturally long neck appears frequently in Carrà's work prior to this.

A drawing of 1912 hints at a natural source for the motif (if such is required) in the cut of a woman's fashionable neckline which (in the drawing) seems to extend the neck vertically some way down the pectoral shelf.[2] The horizontal cut at the base of the neck suggests a sculpture base or the join of a plaster cast such as were common in the academic art schools. Certainly the tension between the dead and the live in an indeterminate interior-exterior space and in a pre-dawn light evokes a dream state with masterly brevity.

No explanation of the title has ever been given, though it seems to share something with the slightly earlier *The Builder's Son* (Collection Massimo Carrà, Milan). To suggest that the square and compasses represent the engineer's profession and the plaster head his secret life impoverishes the richly evocative mystery of the painting. The goal of Metaphysical painting was to make ordinary objects transcend reality and induce an elevated state of consciousness.

The deadpan perspective of the short baton recalls Carrà's admiration for Paolo Uccello, and his claim that his study of early Italian painters from 1914–15 onwards had inspired his abandonment of Futurism in favor of Metaphysical painting.

[1] Illustrated in F. Russoli, M. Carrà, *Carrà. Disegni*, Bologna 1977, pp. 288–89, nos. 393, 399, 400, 401.
[2] The drawing, dated 1912 and in a private collection, is reproduced in V. Fagone (ed.), *Carlo Carrà. La matita e il pennello*, exhibition catalogue, (Accademia Carrara, Bergamo), Milan 1996, p. 183.

Fortunato Depero

11.
PORTRAIT OF CLAVEL,
1917
Oil on canvas,
28 × 30 in. (70 × 75 cm.)

In 1917, the same year that Depero painted this portrait, he described Gilbert Clavel, Swiss poet and art critic, as follows: "a small man, a hunchback, with a rectilinear nose like a triangle, with gold teeth and little feminine shoes, with crystalline and nasal laughter. A man of nerves and will, highly cultured. A professor of Egyptian history, researcher and observer with the sensibility of an artist, writer, a lover of the people, of verse, and of metaphysics. Occasionally I relive in my dreams the lively talk of this beloved poet."[1] Depero did woodcut illustrations for Clavel's short novel, *Un istituto per suicidi* (Bernardo Lux, Rome 1917), and in 1918 they collaborated on Depero's innovative marionette performance *Balli Plastici* (Plastic Dances), which was performed at the Teatro dei Piccoli in Palazzo Odescalchi, Rome.

Depero joined the Futurist movement in 1913 and confirmed his loyalty in 1915 with the manifesto *Futurist Reconstruction of the Universe.* He was even considered the prime exponent of the second generation Futurists, and together with Balla and Marinetti he played a major part in transmitting Futurist ideas and imagery to a younger generation of artists. Nevertheless this painting reveals Depero's distance from first generation Futurist painting, which had been characterized by the exaltation of movement, the interpenetration of planes and the Cubist fragmentation of forms. Influenced instead by the current explorations of the Metaphysical painters and the refined, decorative two-dimensionality of the Viennese Secession, he portrayed Clavel simultaneously in profile and from the front, with flattened and stylized forms. Clavel resembles a wooden marionette painted with the lively colors one might expect of a toy. Like an actor on the stage, frozen in a bizarre perspective framework whose colors render ambiguous the relations between flatness and depth, Depero's Clavel seems the true contemporary of Carrà's mannequins and of Léger's figures.

[1] Quoted in Depero, *Motorumorista Futurista Mimismagico Astrattista Formidabile Architetto e Poeta*, Milan 1986, p. 24.

Amedeo Modigliani

12.
PORTRAIT OF THE PAINTER
FRANK HAVILAND,
1914
Oil on cardboard,
29¼ × 24 in. (73 × 60 cm.)

This vivid portrait, painted in Paris in the second half of 1914, marks Modigliani's return to painting after a period of five years in which he had dedicated himself to sculpture. A slightly smaller oil sketch on board exists in the Los Angeles County Museum of Art,[1] and these two paintings, together with two portraits of Diego Rivera of the same date, share a style of Fauve-inspired unmodulated color in stabbing, broken brushstrokes leaving much of the cardboard support exposed that occurs nowhere else in Modigliani's oeuvre.

The sitter, Frank Burty Haviland, was a wealthy English amateur: a poet, a collector of African art, and a painter of small talent, who occupied a large studio near to Picasso's, and was known disparagingly to his friends as "Le Riche." The red cravat and brown (velvet?) jacket, the aquiline noise, small mouth, and central parting of the hair, with curls, generate the aura of a Wildean aesthete. Placed before a window and with lowered eyes, he contemplates his pipe. Modigliani has surely elongated the curiously bell-shaped head.

[1] O. Patani, *Amedeo Modigliani, Catalogo Generale, Dipinti*, Milan 1991, p. 76, no. 48.

Giorgio Morandi

13.
FLOWERS,
1913
Oil on canvas,
27¼ × 22 in. (68 × 55 cm.)

Painted in the year that Morandi graduated from the Accademia di Belle Arti in Bologna, *Flowers* is among his earliest surviving works, thanks also to the fact that he destroyed many of his paintings at this time. The vigorous and constructive brushwork and the subject itself indicate the overwhelming influence that Cézanne's paintings exercised on the young artist. He is unlikely to have seen any original works by Cézanne prior to the 1914 "Seconda Esposizione della Secessione" in Rome, to which the Galerie Bernheim-Jeune, Paris, lent several paintings. A specific source for *Flowers* may be Vittorio Pica's book on French Impressionist painting, which was published in 1908 and which included a similarly lively *Vase of Flowers* by Cézanne.[1] In addition to the influence of Cézanne, Morandi's awareness of Cubism and of Futurism seems visible even if understated. The subject matter is alien to Futurism and the physical density of the green leaves to Cubism. Nevertheless Morandi's sophisticated awareness of these avant-gardes may have influenced his perception of form and the movement of his brush. The white light intrudes almost physically on the plants and suggests that unification of object and environment that was one of the most firmly held tenets of Boccioni's Futurism at this time. A certain dynamic *furore* rustles the fern leaves. Morandi has fixed his gaze so close to the turbulent arrangement of flowers that the white vase is cut off at the base.

[1] V. Pica, *Gli Impressionisti francesi*, Bergamo 1908, p. 199.

Giorgio Morandi

14.
FRAGMENT,
1914
Oil on canvas,
26⅜ × 12 in. (66 × 30 cm.)

This rare example of a figure in Morandi's work, painted late in 1914, is derived from Cézanne's paintings of *Bathers*, and specifically a painting then in the collection of Egisto Fabbri, Florence, that had been reproduced in a pamphlet on Cézanne published by the Libreria della Voce. It has also been suggested that Morandi's source in the work of Cézanne was transmitted through Picasso —that Morandi had seen a Picasso drawing of *Three Female Nudes* then in the collection of Ardengo Soffici which had been reproduced in the November 1912 issue of *La Voce*.[1] In any case, the photographic origin of the image explains in part Morandi's choice of monochrome, although browns and grays were standard in his palette in this period.

The nude holds up a piece of fabric while another is draped over her left shoulder. The effect of these arching forms around her is to trap her in an overall constructed space in which the distinction between figure and background is diminished. This shows how well Morandi understood Cézanne and how his apprehension in 1914–15 of the Cubism of Picasso and Braque favored precisely the period (1909) when the latter artists

seemed most indebted to Cézanne. The attenuated form of the figure has raised the question of whether Morandi was aware of Derain's work of this period—in which, in a tendency referred to as "gothic," Derain was also stretching heads and bodies into ovals and tubes. It is more likely however that the explanation rests with Morandi's private musings on pictorial form.[2]

Morandi himself cut this painting from a larger canvas, giving it its irregular outline. He then mounted it in on the neutral gray background, giving it an archeological aura, like a salvaged fresco (though we do not know that he intended this).

[1] L. Vitali, *Giorgio Morandi*, Milan 1964, p. 18. The reference is to *La Voce*, IV, 47 (21 November 1912), p. 936.
[2] F. Arcangeli, *Giorgio Morandi*, Milan 1964, pp. 64–5.

Giorgio Morandi

15.
LANDSCAPE,
1914
Oil on canvas,
23¼ × 19¼ in. (58 × 48 cm.)

The luxurious greenery in this view of a house façade almost overwhelmed by trees and hedge rows testifies to Morandi's deeply lyrical empathy with his subject matter. It is likely to be a view of the village of Grizzana, where Morandi's country home was.[1] The viewpoint is from a road looking towards a dark porch, with a staircase leading to an upper story. Persian blinds can be seen on the right.

While the painting, as much as any early work by Morandi, pays homage to the landscapes of Cézanne, it is also possible that Morandi's decision to paint this jungle-like profusion of greenery was prompted by his awareness of the paintings of the late Douanier Rousseau, thanks to a recent publication by the Libreria della Voce, Florence.[2]

[1] F. Russoli (ed.), *Master of Modern Art from the Collection of Gianni Mattioli*, International Exhibitions Foundation, Washington, D.C. 1967, p. 60.
[2] *Dodici opere di Rousseau (Maestri Moderni 2)*, especially no. 11, Florence.

Giorgio Morandi

16.
STILL LIFE WITH CLOCK,
1915
Oil on canvas,
29¾ × 21¼ in. (74.5 × 53 cm.)

The cultural climate in Northern Italy in general, and Ardengo Soffici's articles in *La Voce* in particular, made it inevitable that Morandi was fully aware of Cubism by 1915.

The *Still Life with Clock* is one of several paintings in which Morandi comes close to the cramped, somewhat airless monochrome and faceted paintings of Picasso and Braque circa 1909.

This combination of objects—a clock, two boxes, one on top of each other (possibly a tea caddy and a small book) and a large jug—occur frequently in Morandi's still lifes of this period.

The circular clock face, its mount, and its pedestal are seen from behind and cast a scalloped shadow on the light plane in front of them. The two "boxes" are in the foreground, while the jug, with its high neck and generous lip, is tucked behind.

Despite the Cubist character of this painting, it maintains a firm and comprehensible spatial arrangement, with the table top and background clearly distinguished by a horizontal line. Morandi has, to an unusual degree, crammed his objects into a single complex form. Soon after, he would break them apart and set them in a row before him.

Giorgio Morandi

17.
BOTTLES AND FRUIT-BOWL,
1916
Oil on canvas,
24 × 20 in. (60 × 54 cm.)

The Mantuan oil bottle, the spiral fluted fruit-bowl on a stem, and the elegant tapering white glass bottle have all survived as real objects in Morandi's studio preserved in the Museo Morandi, Bologna. It is a curiosity that the black wedges at the foot of the oil bottle are not shadows but were painted on the bottle itself by Morandi.

Bottles and Fruit-bowl is generally acclaimed as Morandi's first masterpiece: "the first great conquest."[1] The pale cerulean blue of the upper background and the dusty terracotta of the table top are exquisite in their refinement, and their meeting is rendered delicately atmospheric by the white paint scumbled along the "horizon." The *contrapposto* of the vertical fluting of the bottle on the left and the horizontal of the fruit-bowl is scanned by the flat unmodulated white of the obelisk-like bottle in the center. The relative neglect of the chiaroscuro or geometry of the fluting patterns indicates the degree to which Morandi has abandoned any concern with three-dimensional form and focused instead on tonal harmonies and surface pattern.

[1] L. Vitali, *Giorgio Morandi*, Milan 1964, p. 19. This was echoed, for example, by F. Solmi, *Morandi: Storia e leggenda*, Bologna 1978, p. 30. The Mattioli painting is usually coupled with a second still life painted immediately after (dated 23 June 1916), with the same objects but with an additional white bottle (with shoulders and a bulging neck). This was in the collection of Carlo de Frua Angeli, Milan. See L. Vitali, *Morandi. Dipinti. Catalogo Generale*, vol. 1, Milan 1994, no. 29.

Giorgio Morandi

18.
Roses,
1917
Oil on canvas,
23¼ × 20 in. (58 × 50 cm.)

Painted in a year in which Morandi painted only two pictures and was gravely ill for a long period, it is difficult to escape the sensation that this relatively raw still life (compared to *Bottles and Fruit-bowl*), with its harsher colors and broken forms, emanates from Morandi's personal difficulties. Clearly Morandi has tackled a complexity of form in the little nineteenth century vase and the dense red rose buds (with their unnatural reddish leaves) that is absent from his paintings the previous year. Francesco Arcangeli wrote of this painting: "Nothing has changed in the concept compared to the 1916 paintings, except something heated, something disturbing, has insinuated itself into the almost fleshy texture of the painting. The exquisite stillness of 1916 is animated by an almost expressionist jerkiness, the diaphanous pallor is upset by the warmth of a stifling scirocco... The highly elegant heraldry (in the profoundest sense of the word) of 1916 seems to give way, in the exceptionally rare paintings between 1917 and 1918, to an almost animalistic vitality, at the limits of expressionism, which leaps out at one all the more by its contrast with the traditional bipartite two-tone backgrounds."[1] Morandi's source for centralized compositions of flowers in vases like this one has been traced to the Douanier Rousseau, and in particular to an illustration of a painting by Rousseau published by Libreria della Voce in 1914.[2]

[1] F. Arcangeli, *Giorgio Morandi*, Milan 1964, p. 84.
[2] *Dodici opere di Rousseau*, Florence 1914, no. 4.

Ottone Rosai

19.
DYNAMISM BAR SAN MARCO,
1913
Oil on cardboard,
22 × 20⅜ in. (55 × 51 cm.)

One of Rosai's very earliest paintings, this lively and colorful composition with its fragmented planes testifies to his enthusiasm for Futurism, which he encountered in Florence on the occasion of the "Esposizione di pittura futurista di *Lacerba*" at the Galleria Gonnelli (opened 30 November 1913).

Dynamism Bar San Marco was probably painted at the very end of 1913. The Bar San Marco was located in the same street, Via Cavour, as the Galleria Gonnelli, and was a regular meeting place for the *Lacerba* writers and the Futurist artists. The Commedia dell'Arte mask, with its penetrating gaze thanks to a stippled light at the very center of the image, and around which the composition revolves, may refer specifically to Venice (city of San Marco) and to the Venetian carnival. The fracturing of forms and overlapping of planes suggests Rosai's reverence for the Cubo-Futurist style of his fellow-Florentine Ardengo Soffici, although his palette is brighter and blonder than that of either Soffici or Sironi, both of whom were also blending Cubist forms and subjects with Futurist impulsiveness at this time. Rosai's palette and the feathery outlines of his forms resemble those of the contemporary Blaue Reiter painters, August Macke in particular, who enjoyed a relation of reciprocal esteem with the Futurist painters. Rosai followed this painting with a collage of the same subject (Collection Vallecchi, Florence).

Ottone Rosai

20.
FRAGMENTATION OF A STREET,
1914
Oil on canvas,
25¼ × 21¼ in. (63 × 53 cm.)

Together with *Dynamism Bar San Marco, Fragmentation of a Street* is an extremely rare example of Rosai's brief Futurist phase. It bears on the reverse a dedication to the Florentine philosopher and contributor to *Lacerba* Giovanni Papini, and was shown at the Futurist exhibition at the Galleria Sprovieri, Rome, in April 1914 together with *Dynamism Bar San Marco.*

The street is presumably Tuscan, even Florentine, with an arch in alternating colored marble, a vault painted in blue with gold stars, a porch, and carriage wheels going by. A small pasted paper on the left indicates that the street numbers continue within a private courtyard.

The overlapping planes of receding forms, albeit rendered in a fragmentary manner appropriate for the Futurist theme of dynamic movement and crowded visual impressions, anticipate Rosai's treatment of rural architectural forms in his later work. Even the subject, a medieval street, looks forward to Rosai's humble subject matter of village scenes, peasants and vagabonds when in the 1920s, and particularly during his association with the regionalist *Strapaese* group (1926–29), he had abandoned Futurism in favor of simple, even *naif* compositions and an Impressionist technique.

Luigi Russolo

21.
THE SOLIDITY OF FOG,
1912
Oil on canvas,
40 × 26 in. (100 × 65 cm.)

The Futurist painters announced their artistic program in 1910 at a time when they had not yet created a body of work that would fulfill their artistic ambitions and precepts. Luigi Russolo, to a degree greater than any other of the Futurists, systematically attempted to illustrate the images contained in the *Technical Manifesto of Futurist Painting* (April 1910) in oil paintings. *The Solidity of Fog* evokes several passages from the manifesto: "To paint a human figure you must not paint it, you must render the whole of the surrounding atmosphere. Space no longer exists: the street pavement, soaked by rain beneath the glare of an electric lamp, becomes immensely deep and gapes to the very center of the earth ... How is it possible still to see the human face as pink, now that life, redoubled by noctambulism, has multiplied our perceptions as colorists? ... Your eyes, accustomed to semi-darkness, will soon open to more radiant visions of light. The shadows which we shall paint shall be more luminous than the highlights of our predecessors."

As a night scene, *The Solidity of Fog* specifically illustrates the Futurist delight in the electric lighting that permitted a whole new repertoire of visual sensations and experiences in early twentieth century cities: the redoubling of life referred to in the manifesto. The subject, in which atmosphere and mood unite a group of disparate individuals, has a literary equivalent in the so-called "unanimist" poetry current in Paris, with which Marinetti was familiar. For example Jules Romains wrote in *La Vie unanime* (1910): "La rue est plus intime à cause de la brume./ Autour des becs de gaz l'air tout entier s'allume; / Chaque chose a sa part de rayons; /...Les êtres ont fondu leurs formes et leurs vies / Et les âmes se sont doucement asseries. / Je n'ai jamais été moins libre que ce soir / ni moins seul."[1]

The painting is structured by concentric rings radiating from two different points that render tangible the physical sensations of a foggy night. The vague form of a horse drawn carriage is perceptible in the distance. The attempt to paint an equivalent for physical sensation is characteristic of Russolo. Earlier works, for example, took perfume and music as their subjects. Such experiments with synaesthesia link Russolo to the *Scapigliatura* painters of Northern Italy late in the nineteenth century, whose Romantic conviction was also that pictorial technique could convey atmosphere and mood.

[1] Quoted by M. Martin, *Futurist Art and Theory, 1909-15*, Oxford 1968, p. 149, no. 1.

Gino Severini

22.
BLUE DANCER,
1912
Oil on canvas with sequins,
24⅛ × 18⅛ in. (61 x 46 cm.)

The Dance was one of Severini's favorite themes, and was emotively tied, for him, to the café life in Paris that he exalted in his autobiography. Dance-halls and cabarets were numerous in Montmartre and were much frequented by Severini and his artist and writer friends.

Severini painted the *Blue Dancer* together with *The White Dancer* (Civico Museo d'Arte Contemporanea, Jucker Collection, Milan), probably in the second quarter of 1912, in his Paris studio in the Impasse Guelma, where Braque, Dufy, Suzanne Valadon and her son Utrillo also lived. The two paintings were exhibited together and for the first time in the Ridotto of the Teatro Costanzi, Rome, in 1913.

1912 was the year in which Severini came to terms with the Cubism of his friends Picasso and Braque, using it specifically as a means of expressing movement, which was his chief concern at this time. Marianne Martin has written: "The *Blue Dancer* is apparently performing a tango, and the picture is thus 'slower' and much more compact [than *The White Dancer*]. The insistently massed blue suggests the controlled calmness of the dance; the beats are now emphatically linked by appropriately curving forms peculiar to the gestures of this specific dance rhythm."[1] Although the tango was fashionable in Paris from 1907 when Camille de Rhynal made it popular, this was always performed by couples, and a solitary flamenco seems a better description of the mood of the "Danseuse bleu." The dancer, black-haired, with bare arms, is self-absorbed. The jagged splicing of the head contrasts with the softer, curved forms of the billowing blue dress. The café setting is rendered explicit by the red-jacketed waiter, the tables with table cloths, and the fashionably clothed man and woman at the dancer's shoulders.

The effect of movement is in part created by the fusion of the figure with her surroundings by the penetration of light. Flickering light was rendered dazzling by the application of real sequins to the canvas in the areas corresponding to the dress. The immediate inspiration for this was the collage practiced in the previous months by Braque and Picasso, but Severini attributed the idea to a conversation with Apollinaire, who alerted him to the habit of early Italian painters who encrusted their paintings with precious stones and even wooden objects.[2]

Although the depiction of movement and modern life are subjects generally sympathetic to Futurism, it is likely that Severini intended that this should be a variation on Futurist ideas or pictorial iconography. He wrote: "'Inspired by movement' does not mean that

I proposed to render the optical illusion of a thing or body that changes its place in space. My aim was to create, making use of that context, an even newer and more vital whole."[3]

[1] M. Martin, *Futurist Art and Theory, 1909–15*, Oxford 1968, p. 139.
[2] G. Severini, *The Life of a Painter*, trans. J. Franchina, Princeton 1995, p. 117. Severini mentioned specifically Carlo Crivelli's *Camerino triptych* (1482) in the Pinacoteca di Brera, Milan.
[3] *Ibid.*, pp. 104.

Mario Sironi

23.
COMPOSITION WITH PROPELLER,
1915
Tempera and collage on paper,
29¾ × 24⅝ in. (74.5 × 61.5 cm.)

This crowded still life has propeller-like forms both in the vertical brown *papier collé* (an aerial propeller) and in the shiny curves on the right (a marine propeller). Sironi trained as an engineer before turning to painting, and the metallic forms and fragments of tools suggest the Cubist decomposition of a motor. The relevance of the Spanish newspaper clipping in the lower part is unclear.

The energetic brushwork, the celebration of machinery, the spiraling implicit in the propeller(s) as well as the volatile composition, all connect this painting to a Futurist aesthetic strongly conditioned by synthetic Cubism.

Mario Sironi

24.
THE WHITE HORSE,
1919
Oil on canvas,
31⅝ × 23⅝ in. (79 × 59 cm.)

The White Horse combines two moments in Sironi's development as a painter. The upper part resembles the earlier *Composition with Propeller* (cat. no. 23) in its disorder of mechanical or architectonic fragments painted in a rugged Cubist manner. The lower part, with the naked figure and the white horse, has an enigmatic narrative quality that points to Sironi's sympathy for the Metaphysical painting of de Chirico and Carrà. The seemingly wooden figures are closer to Carrà's mannequins than to Depero's dolls. The vague sense of an urban setting which is populated by mythological figures is close to the haunted mood of *pittura metafisica*, but at the same time looks forward to Sironi's characteristic townscapes which he began to paint at about this time. Similarly the deeply etched chiaroscuro and dark palette are marks of Sironi's mature style.

The rough surface of this painting is due in part to the fact that it has been painted, apparently, over an earlier work, probably a Cubist-style collage. This is evidence of the makeshift habits of avant-garde painters at this time, who coped with dire poverty.

Ardengo Soffici

25.
Small Trophy,
1915
Oil on canvas,
18⅝ × 15⅜ in. (46.5 × 38.5 cm.)

The cosmopolitan Florentine critic and painter Ardengo Soffici was probably the closest of the Futurists to Cubism and the Cubists, together with Severini. As early as August 1911 he had written on Picasso and Braque in *La Voce* (the first discussion of Cubism in Italian) and in 1913 his essays were gathered and published as *Cubismo e oltre...* It is not surprising that this elegantly colored small painting has more in common with synthetic Cubism than with Futurist concepts and iconography, in which Soffici seems to have been a reluctant participant between 1912 and 1915.

The gently floating composition of a pipe, a Chianti bottle, and a lemon with a small metal goblet or fruit-dish—the trophy of the title—is suavely lyrical. The stenciled heraldic lilies in the upper part refer perhaps to Florence, Soffici's native city, and the stenciled S to the artist's initial letter.

Ardengo Soffici

26.
FRUIT AND LIQUEURS,
1915
Oil on canvas,
26 × 21⅝ in. (65 × 54 cm.)

This whirling and roughly textured café still life has more of the Futurist spirit in its design than the same artist's earlier *Small Trophy* (cat. no. 25).

The watermelon slices and the shallow fruit bowl are adroitly used to set the composition in motion. The word CHIANTI is reversed in the upper part of the painting, thus deftly throwing into question the viewer's spatial position *vis à vis* the bottles (the letters CHIA appear again in the center). F.C.B. must be the brand name of this particular liqueur and occurs again in a collage by Soffici of the same date. The stenciled letters SOF refer to the artist's name, of course, but may conceivably have more than one meaning.

1915, with the entry of Italy into the Great War, was the year in which Soffici's and Giovanni Papini's journal, *Lacerba*, closed down and in which the Futurists began to disperse. Several of its former adherents began to drift away from Futurist aesthetics and subject matter. The five shining black cherries in the upper left corner herald Soffici's move towards more compact form, realistic drawing and atmospheric painting.

Artists' Biographies

Giacomo Balla
(1871–1958)

Giacomo Balla was born in Turin on 18 July 1871. In 1891 he studied briefly at the Accademia Albertina di Belle Arti and the Liceo Artistico in Turin and exhibited for the first time under the aegis of the Società Promotrice di Belle Arti in that city. He studied at the University of Turin with Cesare Lombroso about 1892. In 1895 Balla moved to Rome, where he worked for several years as an illustrator, caricaturist and portrait painter. In 1899 his work was included in the Venice Biennale and in the "Esposizione Internazionale di Belle Arti" at the galleries of the Società degli Amatori e Cultori di Belle Arti in Rome, where he exhibited regularly for the next ten years. In 1900 Balla spent seven months in Paris assisting the illustrator Serafino Macchiati. About 1903 he began to instruct Gino Severini and Umberto Boccioni in Divisionist painting techniques. In 1903 his work was exhibited at the "Esposizione Internazionale d'Arte della Città di Venezia" and in 1903 and 1904 at the Glaspalast in Munich. In 1904 Balla was represented in the "Internationale Kunstausstellung" in Düsseldorf, and in 1909 exhibited at the "Salon d'Automne" in Paris. Balla signed the second Futurist painting manifesto of 1910 with Boccioni, Carlo Carrà, Luigi Russolo and Severini, although he did not exhibit with the group until 1913. In 1912 he traveled to London and to Düsseldorf, where he began painting his abstract light studies. In 1913 he participated in the "Erste Deutsche Herbstsalon" at the Galerie Der Sturm in Berlin and in an exhibition at the Rotterdamsche Kunstkring in Rotterdam. In 1914 he experimented with sculpture for the first time and showed it in the "Prima Esposizione Libera Futurista" at the Galleria Sprovieri, Rome. He also designed and painted Futurist furniture and designed Futurist "anti-neutral" clothing. With Fortunato Depero, Balla wrote the manifesto *Futurist Reconstruction of the Universe* in 1915. His first solo exhibitions were held that same year at the Società Italiana Lampade Elettriche Z and at the Sala d'Arte A. Angelelli in Rome. His work was also shown in 1915 at the "Panama-Pacific International Exposition" in San Francisco. In 1918 he was given a solo show at the Casa d'Arte Bragaglia in Rome. Balla continued to exhibit in Europe and the United States and in 1935 was made a member of the Accademia di San Luca in Rome. He died on 1 March 1958, in Rome. (L.F.)

Umberto Boccioni
(1882 – 1916)

Umberto Boccioni was born on 19 October 1882 in Reggio Calabria. In 1901 he went to Rome, where he studied design with a sign painter and attended the Scuola Libera del Nudo at the Accademia di Belle Arti. In Rome, he and Gino Severini learned the techniques of Divisionist painting from Giacomo Balla. In 1902 he traveled to Paris, where he studied Impressionist and Neo-Impressionist painting. He participated in the "Mostra dei Rifutati" in 1905 and in the "Esposizione di Belle Arti" in 1906, both in Rome.

Following a trip to Russia in 1906, Boccioni visited Padua and then moved to Venice, where he spent the winter of 1906–7 taking life-drawing classes at the Accademia di Belle Arti. In 1907 he settled in Milan. In 1909–10 he began to frequent the Famiglia Artistica, a Milanese artists' society that sponsored annual exhibitions. During this period he associated with Carlo Carrà and Luigi Russolo, and met Filippo Tommaso Marinetti, who had published the first Futurist manifesto in February of 1909. In 1910 Boccioni participated in the formulation of the two Futurist manifestos: *Manifesto of Futurist Painters* and *Technical Manifesto of Futurist Painting*. Boccioni, Carrà, Russolo and Severini signed the first, and were joined by Balla in signing the second. That same year Boccioni's first solo exhibition was held at Ca' Pesaro in Venice. In the fall of 1911 Boccioni went to Paris, where he met Pablo Picasso and Guillaume Apollinaire through Severini. The same year Boccioni's paintings were shown with those of Carrà, Russolo and Severini in the first Futurist show in Paris, at the Galerie Bernheim-Jeune in 1912. The exhibition then traveled to London, Berlin and Brussels. In 1912 Boccioni began concentrating on sculpture, and his *Technical Manifesto of Futurist Sculpture* was published. From 1912 to 1914 he contributed articles to the Futurist publication *Lacerba*. In 1913 he showed sculpture and paintings in a solo show at the Galerie La Boëtie in Paris, and his sculpture was included in the inaugural exhibition of the Galleria Futurista Permanente in Rome. His book *Pittura scultura futuriste (dinamismo plastico)* appeared in 1914. In July of 1915 Boccioni enlisted in the army with Marinetti, Russolo, and Antonio Sant'Elia. He suffered an accident during cavalry exercises in Sorte near Verona, and died on 17 August 1916. (L.F.)

Carlo Carrà
(1881–1966)

Carrà was born in Quargnento (Alessandria) in 1881. At the age of twelve he left home to work as a mural decorator first at Valenza Po, and from 1895 in Milan. In 1899–1900, Carrà was in Paris decorating pavilions at the "Exposition Universelle," where he became acquainted with contemporary French art. He then spent a few months in London in contact with exiled Italian anarchists, and returned to Milan in 1901. In 1906, he enrolled at the Accademia di Brera in Milan, where he studied under Cesare Tallone. Carrà's work of this time revealed the influence of Italian Divisionism, combined with the frank descriptiveness of nineteenth-century Lombard Naturalism. Carrà met Boccioni and Russolo in 1908 and, after his encounter with Marinetti, on 11 February 1910 signed with them the *Manifesto of Futurist Painters*, followed on 11 April 1910 by the *Technical Manifesto of Futurist Painting*. Carrà's radical political and artistic interests were combined in the monumental painting *Funeral of the Anarchist Galli*, which he reworked after a trip to Paris in the fall of 1911, when he came into direct contact with Cubism. With Ardengo Soffici, Carrà contributed to the Florentine Futurist periodical *Lacerba* (1913–15). In 1914, Carrà was back in Paris where he developed a closer relationship with Apollinaire and Picasso. At that time, he started to work in the medium of collage and words-in-freedom, and endorsed the Italian Interventionist movement in his book *Guerrapittura* of 1915. By 1916, Carrà had rejected many of the nihilistic premises of Futurism. In essays such as "Parlata su Giotto," and "Paolo Uccello costruttore," published in *La Voce* that year, Carrà exalted the art of the Italian Trecento and Quattrocento primitives, for its clarity of form and spiritual dimension. In 1917, he met Giorgio de Chirico in Ferrara and adapted his metaphysical iconography and compositional techniques to a series of bizarre still lifes and interiors. In 1918, Carrà, de Chirico, and his brother Alberto Savinio joined the magazine *Valori Plastici*, edited by Mario Broglio. The following year, he published his book *Pittura metafisica*, which celebrated the transcendent properties of pure form and commonplace objects. Carrà's theoretical position, grounded in a post-war "return to order," signaled his break with the ironic classicism of de Chirico. In addition to his fundamental role as a Futurist, and then as a catalyst for the Italian return to order, Carrà was an influential writer on art: in 1921 he began a seventeen-year tenure as art critic for the Milanese newspaper *L'Ambrosiano*. With *Pine by the Sea* (1920), a painting celebrated by the German critic Wilhelm Worringer, Carrà entered a short-lived phase of Magic Realism. By the mid-twenties, he had evolved his mature style that combined archaizing figures with an atmospheric brushwork, redolent of nineteenth century Impressionist Naturalism. In the 1920s, he participated in the two exhibitions of the *Novecento italiano*, while his interest in the indigenous qualities of the Italian landscape drew him close to the regionalist *Strapaese* group. In the following decade Carrà received commissions for mural paintings under the regime, and signed Mario Sironi's *Manifesto of Mural Painting* in 1933. For the most part, he concentrated on seascapes of the Tuscan coast near Forte dei Marmi. In 1941 he was appointed professor of painting at the Accademia di Brera. In 1945 he published his autobiography *La mia vita*. Carrà died in Milan in 1966. (M.M.)

Fortunato Depero (1892–1960) Depero was born in Fondo (Trento) in 1892 (the region remained a part of Austrian territory until 1918). He studied at the Scuola Reale Elisabettiana in Rovereto. In 1913 he published *Spezzature–Impressioni–Segni e Ritmi*, a book of drawings and poetry in a Symbolist vein. That same year, in Rome, he met Marinetti, Balla and Cangiullo through the Futurist gallery of Giuseppe Sprovieri and became an active member of the Futurist movement, participating in the "Prima Esposizione Libera Futurista" in 1914. In March 1915, he published the manifesto *Futurist Reconstruction of the Universe* with Balla, which included photographs of their "complessi plastici" (plastic complexes)— abstract, kinetic constructions made of ephemeral materials. The manifesto advocated the extension of Futurist research into all fields of design and applied arts and also theorized the representation of psychological and extra-sensorial perceptions. At the outbreak of the war, Depero volunteered for military service but was discharged as unfit. During the war, he composed "onomalingua" (noise songs and poetry purely analogical) and drew plans for Futurist visionary architecture. In 1916–17, Depero met Sergej Diaghilev and was commissioned to do set designs and costumes for *The Song of the Nightingale* by Igor Stravinsky. Although never realized, it marked the beginning of Depero's long involvement with theater. At the same time, he collaborated with the Swiss writer Gilbert Clavel on the choreography and sets of *Balli Plastici* (Plastic Dances) performed in Rome, at the Teatro dei Piccoli in 1918. In his own paintings, Depero depicted a fantastic world of vegetal, animal and mechanical forms, in a dynamic synthesis of large, flat areas of bright color. Depero, together with Balla, was largely responsible for the artistic development of Futurism in its post-war phase. In 1919 he founded the Casa d'Arte Futurista in Rovereto, where he produced furniture, objects, graphics, posters and tapestries, with his wife Rosetta. In 1921–22 he furnished the Cabaret del Diavolo in the Hôtel élite et des étrangers in Rome. In 1925–26, Depero spent eighteen months in Paris, where he showed in the Italian pavilion of the "Exposition Internationale des Arts Decoratifs et Industriels Modernes," with Balla and Prampolini. Depero experimented with built structures designed out of letters—what he termed "typographical" or "advertising architecture." He realized his most famous example at the "Seconda Biennale Internazionale d'Arte Decorativa" in

Monza, 1927, with the book pavilion for the publishers Bestetti, Tumminelli and Treves in the form of monumental letters. In the early 1930s he did a similar project for the Campari factory, and designed several famous advertising campaigns for the same liquor company. In 1932 he authored the *Manifesto of Advertising Art*. From the late 1920s he lived in New York, where he designed the Enrico and Paglieri (1929) and Zucca (1930–31) restaurants. In 1929–30, he also designed vertiginous scenes of metropolitan life for the sets of *The New Babel* performed by the American Sketches ballet. Mostly, however, he worked as graphic designer for important magazines, notably *Vanity Fair*. He continued this activity in Italy, designing covers for *Emporium*, *La Rivista* (1927) and *Vogue* (1929). He also contributed to newspapers and magazines, such as *La sera*, *Illustrazione Italiana*, *Secolo Illustrato* and others, and in 1933 he published five issues of the Futurist magazine *Dinamo Futurista*. In 1934, he published *Liriche radiofoniche* (Radio Lyrics), which were created specifically to be broadcasted on the radio. After the Second World War, Depero continued with commissions for large-scale decorations. He died in Rovereto in 1960. (M.M.)

Amedeo Modigliani
(1884–1920)

Amedeo Modigliani was born on 12 July 1884 in Livorno. The serious illnesses he suffered during his childhood persisted throughout his life. At age fourteen he began to study painting. He first experimented with sculpture during the summer of 1902 and the following year attended the Regio Istituto di Belle Arti in Venice. Early in 1906 Modigliani went to Paris where he settled in Montmartre and attended the Académie Colarossi. His early work was influenced by Toulouse-Lautrec, Théophile-Alexandre Steinlen, Gauguin and Cézanne. In the autumn of 1907 he met his first patron, Dr. Paul Alexandre, who purchased works from him before World War I. Modigliani exhibited in the "Salon d'Automne" in 1907 and 1912 and in the "Salon des Indépendants" in 1908, 1910 and 1911. In 1909 Modigliani met Brancusi when both artists lived in Montparnasse. From 1909 to 1915 he concentrated on sculpture but he also drew and painted to a certain extent. However, the majority of his paintings date from 1916 to 1919. Modigliani's circle of friends first consisted of Max Jacob, Lipchitz and the Portuguese sculptor Amedeo de Souza-Cardoso and later included Chaim Soutine, Maurice Utrillo, Jules Pascin, Foujita, Moïse Kisling and the Sitwells. His dealers were Paul Guillaume (1914–16) and Leopold Zborowski (by 1917). The only one-man show given the artist during his lifetime took place at the Galerie Berthe Weill in December 1917. In March 1917 Modigliani met Jeanne Hébuterne who became his companion and model. From March or April 1918 until May 1919, they lived in the south of France, in both Nice and Cagnes. Modigliani died in Paris on 24 January 1920. (V.E.B.)

Giorgio Morandi
(1890-1964)

Morandi was born in Bologna in 1890. At the age of sixteen, he went to work in his father's commercial office, but in 1907 he also enrolled at the Accademia di Belle Arti in Bologna, where he graduated in 1913. Morandi was influenced by the Italian masters Giotto, Paolo Uccello, Masaccio and Piero della Francesca, but also by Vermeer, Chardin, Corot and especially Cézanne. Throughout his career, Morandi produced almost exclusively still lifes and landscapes (with the exception of a few self-portraits). In 1914, he briefly digressed into a Futurist style and also exhibited at the second Rome Secession. In that same year, Morandi was appointed instructor of drawing for elementary schools in

Bologna—a post he held until 1929. In 1915, he joined the army but suffered a breakdown and was indefinitely discharged. During the war, Morandi's still lifes became more reduced in their compositional elements and purer in form, revealing his admiration for both Cézanne and the Douanier Rousseau. Morandi knew de Chirico's and Carrà's work through reproductions in the journal *La Raccolta*. Edited by Morandi's fellow Bolognese, Giuseppe Raimondi, *La Raccolta* represented the post-war attitude of a "return to order" and to traditional artistic craft, and was the first to recognize Morandi's work. In 1918, Morandi became affiliated with the journal *Valori Plastici* and his work was included in the group's exhibition which traveled throughout Germany in 1921. During the period of *Valori Plastici* Morandi painted a series of enigmatic still lifes with starkly-modeled objects immobilized in an anti-naturalistic space and light. In the catalogue essay for the exhibition of the "Fiorentina Primaverile" in 1922, de Chirico defined Morandi's work as the "metaphysics of everyday objects." By the early twenties Morandi's art had abandoned any reference to Metaphysical painting, and focused increasingly on subtle gradations of hue, tone, and objects arranged in a unifying atmospheric haze. Morandi showed in the *Novecento italiano* exhibitions of 1926 and 1929, but was more specifically associated with the regionalist *Strapaese* group by the end of the decade. In 1927 he exhibited at the "Seconda esposizione dell'incisione moderna" in Florence. His work was widely reproduced and discussed by the *Strapaese* critics Mino Maccari and Leo Longanesi in the journals *Il Selvaggio* and *L'Italiano*. They considered him the quintessential Italian artist: he embodied independence from European currents and an appreciation of Italian small-town life, as epitomized in the consistency and simplicity of his still lifes. Morandi was devoted to the medium of etching, and increasingly so from the late twenties. From 1930 to 1956, he was professor of printmaking at the Accademia di Belle Arti in Bologna. In 1935, in *Momenti della pittura bolognese*, Roberto Longhi defined him as "one of the best living painters in Italy," a reputation that continued in the post-war years as Morandi was additionally perceived as one of the few artists to have escaped the taint of Fascism, and to have evolved a style of pure pictorial values congenial to modernist abstraction. Morandi visited Paris for the first time in 1956. He died in Bologna in 1964. (M.M.)

Ottone Rosai
(1895–1957)

Rosai was born in 1895 in a working-class neighborhood of Florence. His father was a carpenter. In 1909–12, Rosai studied at the Accademia of Florence and in his early years admired the work of Corot, Courbet, Cézanne and Daumier. In 1913 Rosai, with his friend Betto Lotti, showed a group of works in Florence in Via Cavour, in a site next to the Futurist exhibition organized by *Lacerba*. His show was visited by Marinetti, Soffici, Carrà and other Futurists. Rosai then joined the Futurist movement and experimented with polimaterism in his art. He also contributed to *Lacerba*. During World War I, Rosai volunteered in the *Arditi*, the daring assault troops, and was wounded several times. In the post-war years he participated in the creation and in the activities of the local Fascist squads. In 1919 he published his first book *Il libro di un teppista*. His disillusionment with Fascism began with Giacomo Matteotti's murder in 1924, and was furthered after the establishment of the regime. In 1920, Rosai held his first one-man show in Florence, which was favorably reviewed by de Chirico and Soffici. In the post-war years, Rosai's art combined the simple forms and suspended mood of Metaphysical painting with a naturalist, atmospheric brushwork. His subject matter focused on the popular neighborhoods of Florence and their working class inhabitants.

His strong sense of realism, solidly grounded in folk tradition, was often pushed to the verge of caricature. In 1926, Rosai showed in the exhibition of the *Novecento italiano*. In 1929 he began contributing illustrations to the Fascist periodical *Il Bargello*. In 1930 the Milanese Galleria Il Milione opened with a one-man show of his work. In the same year Rosai published his second novel, *Via Toscanella,* and in 1934, his third, *Dentro la guerra*. In 1939, he was appointed professor of drawing at the Liceo Artistico Fiorentino. Rosai died in 1957 in Ivrea, while there for the opening of a large retrospective at the Centro Culturale d'Ivrea. (M.M.)

Luigi Russolo
(1885–1947)

Russolo was born in Portogruaro (Venice) in 1885. His father was the local cathedral organist and director of the Schola Cantorum at Latisana. While his two older brothers graduated from the Milan conservatory, Russolo, after joining his family in Milan in 1901, chose to pursue painting. In 1909 he showed a group of etchings at the Famiglia Artistica in Milan, where he met Boccioni and Carrà. His Divisionist period works were influenced by Previati and particularly by Boccioni in style and subject matter. The following year, after his encounter with Marinetti, Russolo signed both the *Manifesto of Futurist Painters* and the *Technical Manifesto of Futurist Painting*. Afterwards, he participated in all Futurist soirées and exhibitions. His mature Futurist canvases, while open to Cubist influence, drew primarily on the examples of Anton Giulio Bragaglia's photo-dynamism and Etienne-Jules Marey's chrono-photography. On 11 March 1913, Russolo issued his manifesto *L'arte dei rumori* (The Art of Noises), dedicated to fellow Futurist composer Francesco Balilla Pratella. Expanded into book form in 1916, it theorized the inclusion of incidental noise into musical composition. With Ugo Piatti, he later invented the *intonarumori*, noise-emitting machines that allowed for the modification of tone and pitch. In 1913–14, Russolo conducted his first Futurist concerts with numerous *intonarumori*. Audiences in Milan, Genoa and London reacted with enthusiasm or open hostility. Russolo started to contribute to the magazine *Lacerba*, where in 1914 he published his "Grafia enarmonica per gl'intonarumori" (Enharmonic Notation for Futurist Intonarumori), which introduced a new and influential form of musical notation. With the outbreak of the war, Russolo volunteered, like many of his Futurist friends, in the Lombard Volunteer Cyclists Battalion. After being seriously wounded in December 1917, he spent eighteen months in various hospitals. In 1921 Russolo held three concerts in Paris with an orchestra of twenty-seven *intonarumori*. The performances were greatly acclaimed by Stravinsky, Diaghilev (who had already applauded him in Milan in 1915), Ravel, and Mondrian, who devoted a long article to the *intonarumori* in *De Stijl*. Due to his opposition to Fascism, Russolo spent most of his time between 1927 and 1932 in Paris. Beginning in 1922, he invented a series of *rumorarmoni*, a kind of harmonium which allowed for the extension of tone and pitch by the simple shift of one register. In 1925 he patented the "enharmonic bow" and later the "enharmonic piano." Russolo appeared in three short Futurist films (now lost), for which he also composed the music. He held his last concert in 1929, presented by Edgard Varèse, at the opening of a Futurist show in Paris at the Galerie 23. In 1931 he moved to Tarragona in Spain, where he studied occult philosophy and then in 1933 returned to Italy, settling in Cerro di Laveno on Lake Maggiore. Russolo published his philosophical investigations *Al di là della materia* (Beyond Matter) in 1938. In 1941–42, he took up painting again in a realist style that he called "classic-modern." Russolo died at Cerro di Laveno in 1947. (M.M.)

Gino Severini
(1883–1966)

Gino Severini was born on 7 April 1883 in Cortona. He studied at the Scuola Tecnica in Cortona before moving to Rome in 1899, where he attended art classes at the Villa Medici. By 1901 he met Umberto Boccioni, who had also recently arrived in Rome, and together they visited the studio of Giacomo Balla, who introduced them to Divisionist painting. After settling in Paris in November 1906, Severini studied Impressionist painting and met the Neo-Impressionist Paul Signac. He soon came to know most of the Parisian avant-garde, including Georges Braque, Juan Gris, Amedeo Modigliani and Pablo Picasso, Lugné-Poe and his theatrical circle, the poets Guillaume Apollinaire, Paul Fort and Max Jacob and author Jules Romains. After joining the Futurist movement at the invitation of Filippo Tommaso Marinetti and Boccioni, Severini signed the *Technical Manifesto of Futurist Painting* of 11 April 1910, along with Balla, Boccioni, Carlo Carrà and Luigi Russolo. However, Severini was less attracted to the subject of the machine than his fellow Futurists and frequently chose the form of the dancer to express Futurist theories of dynamism in art. In February 1912 Severini helped organized the first Futurist exhibition at the Galerie Bernheim-Jeune, Paris, and participated in subsequent Futurist shows in Europe and the United States. In 1913 he had solo exhibitions at the Marlborough Gallery, London, and Der Sturm, Berlin. During his Futurist period Severini acted as an important link between artists in France and Italy. After his last truly Futurist works—a series of paintings on war themes—Severini painted in a Synthetic Cubist mode, and by 1920 he was applying theories of classical balance based on the golden section to figurative subjects from the traditional Commedia dell'Arte. After 1920 he divided his time between Paris and Rome. During the 1920s he explored fresco and mosaic techniques and executed murals in various mediums in Switzerland, France and Italy. In the 1950s he returned to the subjects of his Futurist years: dancers, light and movement. Throughout his career Severini published important theoretical essays and books on art. Severini died in Paris on 16 February 1966. (L.F.)

Mario Sironi
(1885–1961)

Sironi was born on 12 May 1885 in Sassari. His father, an engineer, moved the family back to Rome the following year. In 1902 Sironi enrolled in the engineering school at the University of Rome, but soon abandoned his studies. At the Scuola Libera del Nudo, which he began attending in 1903, Sironi met Giacomo Balla, Umberto Boccioni, and Gino Severini. He exhibited at the "Esposizione della Società degli Amatori e Cultori" in 1905, and contributed illustrations to the Socialist journal *L'Avanti della Domenica*. He travelled to Paris in 1906 (where he roomed with Boccioni), Munich in 1908, and Frankfurt in 1910. Suffering from depression, he spent long periods of his youth in seclusion and destroyed most of his early, Divisionist work. At the encouragement of Boccioni, Sironi began to adhere to Futurism late in 1913, participating in the "Esposizione Libera Futurista" at the Galleria Sprovieri in 1914. By 1915 Sironi had moved to Milan, and, at the invitation of Filippo Tommaso Marinetti, took the place of Ardengo Soffici in the core Futurist group. That same year he signed the Futurist interventionist manifesto *L'orgoglio italiano* (Italian Pride). He served at the front with Marinetti, Boccioni, Luigi Russolo, and Antonio Sant'Elia. He continued his work as an illustrator, primarily for the Futurist cultural weekly, *Gli Avvenimenti*, in Milan. In 1919 Sironi participated in the "Grande Mostra Futurista" in Milan, organized by Marinetti as a show of the movement's strength in the immediate post-war period. Yet Sironi was already turning away from the Futurist abrtraction in favor of a figurative style and clearly delineated form. That same year he held his first one-man show at the Casa d'Arte Bragaglia in Rome. In 1920 he signed *Contro tutti i ritorni in pittura* (Against All Revivals in Painting) with Russolo and other former Futurists: the manifesto argued for a return to pure pictorial values, but without the slavish imitation of the Quattrocento primitives represented by *Valori Plastici*. From 1919–21 he painted his famous series of *paesaggi urbani,* urban landscapes, which transformed de Chirico's haunting Italian *piazze d'Italia*, city-squares, into contemporary scenes of the Milanese industrial periphery. During the same period he made his reputation as a political commentator in his illustrations for *Le Industrie Italiane Illustrate*. In 1922 he was one of the founding members of the *Sette di Novecento* in Milan and became the leading exponent of the *Novecento italiano*. Sironi was the chief political caricaturist and illustrator for Mussolini's official press, *Il Popolo d'Italia* (1927–33) and *La Rivista Illustrata del Popolo d'Italia* (1934–39). He was also the leading theorist and practitioner of mural painting and received prominent commissions from the regime. He authored the influential *Manifesto of Mural Painting* in 1933. After World War II he returned to easel painting in a style consistent with the abstract Informel movement. In 1956 he was elected member of the Accademia di San Luca. Sironi died in Milan on 13 August 1961. (E.B.)

Ardengo Soffici (1879–1964) Soffici was born in Rignano sull'Arno (Florence) in 1879. In 1892, at the age of thirteen, he moved to Florence with his family. Due to the death of his father, at nineteen, he had to start work at a lawyer's office. He also briefly attended the Florence Academy until he left for Paris in 1900. Attending the soirées at the Caveau of the Soleil d'Or led by the Greek poet Jean Moreás, Soffici met Guillaume Apollinaire and through him, Pablo Picasso, Georges Braque, Max Jacob, and André Salmon. He worked as an illustrator for *La Plume*, *La Revue Blanche* and *L'assiette au beurre*. After 1903, he began to return to Italy for the summer, staying mostly in Poggio a Caiano, where he met Giuseppe Prezzolini and Giovanni Papini, then editors of *Leonardo*. In 1907, he settled in Italy and the following year began as a regular contributor, along with Papini, to Prezzolini's journal *La Voce*. He designed the masthead and served as the art critic, championing current French art as well as Medardo Rosso and Giovanni Segantini to the reading public. From the pages of *La Voce,* in 1910, he harshly criticized Futurism. Soffici also organized an influential show of little-known French Impressionist painting in Florence. In 1909 *Ignoto toscano* (The Unknown Tuscan), his first literary work, was published; in 1910 his book *Arthur Rimbaud* appeared, and in 1912 the autobiographic novel *Lemmonio Boreo*. Soffici spent most of 1912 in Paris, often in the company of Gino Severini. In search of a more radical stance, Soffici and Papini broke from *La Voce* in 1913 and founded the magazine *Lacerba*, which became the mouthpiece of Florentine Futurism. In that year, *Lacerba* sponsored the first exhibition of Futurist art in Florence. He became an active member of the Futurist movement, taking part in soirées and exhibitions in Italy and abroad, although he maintained his distance from Marinetti and his commitment gradually began to wane. In 1914, Soffici published *Cubismo e futurismo* (Cubism and Futurism) and in the following year, *BIF & ZF + 18*, a text inspired by Apollinaire's *Calligrammes*. *Lacerba* supported Italy's Interventionist movement and Soffici volunteered. However, upon Italy's entry into the war, the magazine folded. He later published his war-time experiences in the autobiographic novels *Kobilek* (1918) and *La ritirata del Friuli* (1919). After the war, Soffici advocated a return to solid and "classical" principles and values. He contributed to *Valori Plastici*, and in 1920 he founded his own, short-lived magazine *Rete Mediterranea* in support of an art that was "healthy, wise and serene." The first monograph on Soffici was written by Carrà and published by *Valori Plastici* in 1922. Soffici served as a father figure to the younger artists and critics of *Il Selvaggio* and *L'Italiano*, where he also published articles supporting the ruralist and nationalistic movement of *Strapaese*. Soffici became a leading theorist of a Fascist art, publishing his essays in the collection *Periplo dell'arte–Richiamo all'ordine* in 1928, where he attempted a reconciliation between the avant-garde and the modes and values of a "rappel à l'ordre." His own work consisted of still lifes, landscapes and peasant scenes from his native Tuscany, rendered in a conservative naturalist-realist style. Soffici died in Forte dei Marmi (Lucca) in 1964. (M.M.)

Further Reading

Giacomo Balla

Giacomo Balla. Opere dal 1912 al 1928, Tunske & Tunske, Zurich 1985.

M. Fagiolo dell'Arco, *Balla: Ricostruzione Futurista dell'Universo*, Bulzoni, Rome 1968.

M. Fagiolo dell'Arco, *Futur-Balla: la vita e le opere*, Electa, Milan 1982.

M. Fagiolo dell'Arco, *Balla: the Futurist*, Museum of Modern Art, Oxford 1987.

M. Fagiolo dell'Arco, *Balla e i futuristi*, Electa, Milan 1988.

G. Lista, *Balla*, Galleria Fonte d'Abisso, Modena 1982.

Umberto Boccioni

Umberto Boccioni. Dinamismo di un cavallo in corsa + case, exhibition catalogue, Peggy Guggenheim Collection, Venice 1996.

G. Ballo, *Boccioni*, Il Saggiatore, Milan 1964 (2nd ed. 1982).

G. Ballo, *Boccioni a Milano*, exhibition catalogue (Palazzo Reale, Milan), Mazzotta, Milan 1982.

G. Ballo, L. De Maria, F. Russoli, *Boccioni e il suo tempo*, exhibition catalogue (Palazzo Reale, Milan), Ed. Arti Grafiche Fiorini, Milan 1973.

Z. Birolli (ed.), *Umberto Boccioni. Gli Scritti editi e inediti*, Feltrinelli, Milan 1971.

M. Calvesi, *Boccioni prefuturista*, exhibition catalogue (Museo Nazionale di Reggio Calabria), Electa, Milan 1983.

M. Calvesi, E. Coen, *Boccioni. L'opera completa*, Electa, Milan 1983.

E. Coen, *Umberto Boccioni*, exhibition catalogue, The Metropolitan Museum of Art, New York 1988.

L. Mattioli Rossi (ed.), *Boccioni 1912 Materia*, exhibition catalogue (Fondazione A. Mazzotta, Milan), Mazzotta, Milan 1995.

Carlo Carrà

M. Carrà (ed.), *Carlo Carrà: Tutta l'opera pittorica*, 3 vols., Edizioni dell'Annunciata; Edizioni della Conchiglia, Milan 1967–68.

M. Carrà (ed.), *Carlo Carrà. Tutti gli scritti*, Feltrinelli, Milan 1976.

G.A. Dell'Acqua, G. Briganti, E. Coen, M. Garberi, *Carrà*, Palazzo Reale, Milan 1987.

M. Fagiolo dell'Arco, M. Carrà, *Carlo Carrà: Il Primitivismo,*

1915–1919, Mazzotta, Milan
1987.

V. Fagone (ed.), *Carlo Carrà: la
matita e il pennello*, exhibition
catalogue (Accademia Carrara,
Bergamo), Skira, Milan 1996.

A. Monferini (ed.), *Carlo Carrà,
1881–1966*, Galleria Nazionale
d'Arte Moderna, Rome 1994.

Fortunato Depero
G. Belli, *Depero: dal Futurismo
alla Casa d'arte*, exhibition
catalogue (Palazzo delle
Esposizioni, Rome), Charta,
Milan 1994.

B. Passamani (ed.), *Fortunato
Depero, 1892–1960*, Museo
Civico, Bassano del Grappa
1970.

B. Passamani (ed.), *Fortunato
Depero*, Musei Civici, Galleria
Museo Depero, Rovereto 1981.

M. Scudiero, D. Lieber (eds.),
*Depero Futurista & New York: il
Futurismo e l'arte pubblicitaria*,
Musei Civici, Galleria Museo
Depero, Rovereto 1986.

Amedeo Modigliani
Amedeo Modigliani 1884–1920,
exhibition catalogue, Musée d'art
moderne de la Ville de Paris,
Paris 1981.

A. Ceroni, F. Cachin, *Tout
l'œuvre peint de Modigliani*, Paris
1972.

C. Mann, *Modigliani*, Thames
and Hudson, London 1980.

O. Patani, *Amedeo Modigliani.
Catalogo generale. Dipinti*,
Leonardo, Milan 1991.

Giorgio Morandi
Morandi e il suo tempo,
exhibition catalogue (Galleria
Comunale di Arte Moderna,
Bologna), Mazzotta, Milan 1985.

F. Arcangeli, *Giorgio Morandi*,
Edizioni del Milione, Milan
1964.

L. Vitali, *Morandi. Catalogo
generale*, 2 vols., Electa, Milan
1977 (revised ed. 1983).

J.M. Lukach (ed.), *Giorgio
Morandi: 20th Century Modern*,
exhibition catalogue, The
Solomon R. Guggenheim
Museum, New York 1981.

M. Pasquali, L. Selleri, *Museo
Morandi, Bologna: il catalogo*,
Charta, Milan 1993.

Ottone Rosai
C. Bo (ed.), *Vecchio autoritratto*,
[includes Ottone Rosai, *Il libro
di un teppista* (1919), *Via
Toscanella* (1930), *Dentro la
guerra* (1934)], Vallecchi,
Florence 1951.

L. Cavallo, *Ottone Rosai*,
Edizioni Galleria il Castello,
Milan 1973.

P.C. Santini, *Ottone Rosai: Opere
dal 1911 al 1957*, Vallecchi,
Florence 1983.

V. Corti (ed.), *Ottone Rosai,
"Nient'altro che un artista,"*
Tracc Edizioni, Piombino 1987.

Luigi Russolo
M.R. Zanovello, U. Nebbia,
P. Buzzi, *Russolo: l'uomo, l'artista*,
C. Corticelli, Milan 1958.

G. Maffina, *L'Opera grafica di
Luigi Russolo*, Ceal, Varese 1977.

G. Maffina, *Luigi Russolo e l'arte
dei rumori, con tutti gli scritti
musicali*, Martano, Turin 1978.

D. Collovini, *Luigi Russolo:
un'appendice al futurismo,*

exhibition catalogue, Supernova, Venice 1997.

Gino Severini

R. Barilli (ed.), *Gino Severini*, exhibition catalogue (Palazzo Pitti, Florence), Electa, Florence 1983.

M. Fagiolo dell'Arco, E. Coen, *Un taccuino cubo-futurista*, Bulzoni, Rome 1977.

D. Fonti, *Severini. Catalogo ragionato*, Mondadori, Milan 1988.

G. Severini, *Tutta la vita di un pittore*, Garzanti, Milan 1946 (reprinted Feltrinelli, Milan 1983). English ed., trans. James Franchina, *The Life of a Painter*, Princeton University Press, Princeton 1995.

G. Severini, *Ecrits sur l'art*, Editions Cercle d'Art, Paris 1987.

Mario Sironi

Mario Sironi, exhibition catalogue (Palazzo Reale, Milan), Electa, Milan 1973.

Mario Sironi, exhibition catalogue (Stadtische Kunsthalle, Düsseldorf), DuMont, Cologne 1988.

Mario Sironi 1885–1961, exhibition catalogue (Galleria Nazionale d'Arte Moderna, Rome), Electa, Milan 1993.

E. Braun, "Mario Sironi's Urban Landscapes: The Futurist/Fascist Nexus," in M. Antliff and M. Affron (eds.), *Fascist Visions: Art and Ideology in France and Italy*, Princeton University Press, Princeton 1997.

F. Benzi, A. Sironi, *Sironi Illustratore. Catalogo ragionato*, De Luca, Rome 1988.

M. Penelope (ed.), *Sironi. Opere 1902–1960*, Mondadori and De Luca, Milan and Rome 1985.

Ardengo Soffici

A. Soffici, *Autoritratto d'artista italiano nel quadro del suo tempo*. 4 vols., Vallecchi, Florence 1951 (I), 1952 (II), 1954 (III), 1955 (IV).

A. Soffici, *Opere*, 7 vols., Vallecchi Editore, Florence 1959 (I–II), 1960 (III), 1961 (IV), 1963 (V), 1965 (VI), 1968 (VII t.1–t.2).

L. Cavallo, *Soffici immagini e documenti*, Vallecchi, Florence1986.

L. Corsetti, M. Moretti (eds.), *Nuovi contributi critici su Ardengo Soffici*, Quaderni Sofficiani, 1, Poggio a Caiano 1994.

Photograph Credits

Color photographs have been supplied by the Gianni Mattioli Collection.

Black and white photographs for the essay "Gianni Mattioli" have been supplied by Laura Mattioli Rossi.

Black and white photographs for the essay "Renaissance and Renascences: The Rebirth of Italy, 1911–1921" have been supplied by: Archivi Alinari–Istituto Luce; Archivio Storico delle Arti Contemporanee, Ente Autonomo La Biennale di Venezia; Archivio Storico del Museo della Didattica, III Università di Roma; The Beinecke Rare Book and Manuscript Library, Yale University Library, New Haven, Connecticut; Biblioteca Nazionale Centrale, Florence (Alfa Fotostudio); Fondazione Primo Conti–Centro di documentazione e ricerche sulle Avanguardie storiche, Fiesole (Florence); Fondazione "Il Vittoriale degli Italiani," Gardone Riviera (Brescia); Galleria dello Scudo, Verona; Luce Marinetti, Rome; Soprintendenza per i Beni Artistici e Storici del Veneto, Ministero per i Beni Culturali e Ambientali, Rome.

This volume was printed by Elemond S.p.a.
at the plant in Martellago (Venice) in 1997